Important Instru

Students, Parents, and Teachers can use the URL or QR code provided below to access Lumos back to school refresher online assessment. Please note that this assessment is provided in the Online format only.

URL
Visit the URL below and place the book access code **http://www.lumoslearning.com/a/tedbooks** **Access Code: BS89E-14852-P**
OR **Scan the QR code with your Smartphone** 

Lumos Learning
Developed by Expert Teachers

Lumos Back-to-School Refresher tedBook - 9th Grade English Language Arts, Back to School book to address Summer Slide designed for classroom and home use

Contributing Editor	-	**Erin Schollaert**
Contributing Editor	-	**Nina Anderson**
Contributing Editor	-	**George Smith**
Executive Producer	-	**Mukunda Krishnaswamy**
Designer and Illustrator	-	**Vagesh Kumar**

First Edition - 2020

NGA Center/CCSSO are the sole owners and developers of the Common Core State Standards, which does not sponsor or endorse this product. © Copyright 2010. National Governors Association Center for Best Practices and Council of Chief State School Officers.

ISBN-13: 978-1-082808-82-1

Printed in the United States of America

For permissions and additional information contact us

Lumos Information Services, LLC
PO Box 1575, Piscataway, NJ 08855-1575
http://www.LumosLearning.com

Email: support@lumoslearning.com
Tel: (732) 384-0146
Fax: (866) 283-6471

Developed by Expert Teachers

Table of Contents

INTRODUCTION

This book is specifically designed to help diagnose and remedy Summer Learning Loss in students who are starting their ninth-grade classes. It provides a comprehensive and efficient review of 8th Grade English Language Arts standards through an online assessment. Before starting ninth-grade instruction, parents/teachers can administer this online test to their students. After the students complete the test, a standards mastery report is immediately generated to pinpoint any proficiency gaps. Using the diagnostic report and the accompanying study plan, students can get targeted remedial practice through lessons included in this book to overcome any Summer learning loss.

Addressing the Summer slide during the first few weeks of a new academic will help students have a productive ninth-grade experience.

The online program also gives your student an opportunity to briefly explore various standards that are included in the 9th grade curriculum.

Some facts about Summer Learning Loss
- Students often lose an average of 2 and ½ months of math skills
- Students often lose 2 months of reading skills
- Teachers spend at least the first 4 to 5 weeks of the new school year reteaching important skills and concepts

Lumos Learning Back-To-School Refresher Methodology
The following graphic shows the key components of the Lumos back-to-school refresher program.

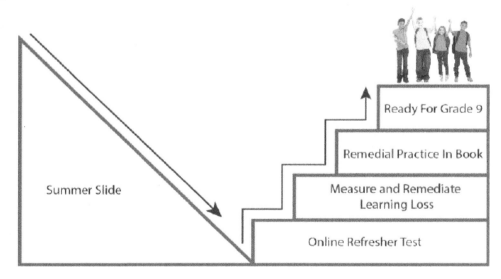

Chapter 1
How to Use this Book Effectively

Step 1: Access Online Diagnostic Assessment

Use the URL and access code provided below or scan the QR code to access the Diagnostic assessment and get started. The online diagnostic test helps to measure the summer loss and remediate loss in an efficient and effective way.

After completing the test, your student will receive immediate feedback with detailed reports on standards mastery. With this report, use the next section of the book to design a practice plan for your student to overcome the summer loss.

URL	QR Code
Visit the URL below and place the book access code **http://www.lumoslearning.com/a/tedbooks** **Access Code: BS89E-14852-P**	

Step 2: Review the Personalized Study Plan Online

After you complete the online practice test, access your individualized study plan from the table of contents (Figure 2)

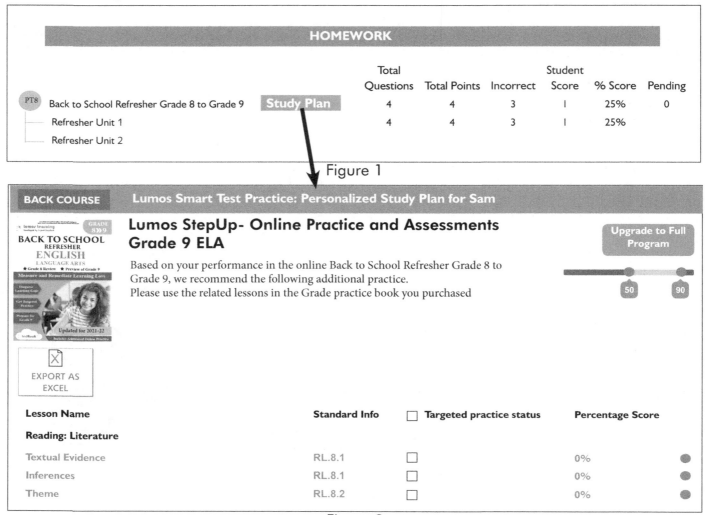

HOMEWORK

	Total Questions	Total Points	Incorrect	Student Score	% Score	Pending
PT8 Back to School Refresher Grade 8 to Grade 9 — **Study Plan**	4	4	3	1	25%	0
Refresher Unit 1	4	4	3	1	25%	
Refresher Unit 2						

Figure 1

BACK COURSE   Lumos Smart Test Practice: Personalized Study Plan for Sam

Lumos StepUp- Online Practice and Assessments Grade 9 ELA

Upgrade to Full Program

50   90

Based on your performance in the online Back to School Refresher Grade 8 to Grade 9, we recommend the following additional practice.
Please use the related lessons in the Grade practice book you purchased

EXPORT AS EXCEL

Lesson Name	Standard Info	☐ Targeted practice status	Percentage Score	
Reading: Literature				
Textual Evidence	RL.8.1	☐	0%	●
Inferences	RL.8.1	☐	0%	●
Theme	RL.8.2	☐	0%	●

Figure 2

Step 3: Remediate Summer Learning Loss

Using the information provided in the study plan report, complete the targeted practice using the appropriate lessons in this book to overcome Summer learning loss. Using the Lesson Name, find the appropriate practice lessons in this book and answer the questions provided. After completing the practice in the book you can mark the progress in your study plan as shown the figure 2.

Chapter 2 - Reading: Literature

The objective of the Reading Literature standards is to ensure that the student is able to read and comprehend literature (which includes stories, drama and poetry) related to the grade. We encourage the student to go through the resources available online on Lumos EdSearch to gain an in depth understanding of the related concepts. A small mind map is provided after each passage or text in which the student can enter the details as understood from the literary text. Doing this will help the student to refer to key points that help in answering the questions with ease.

RL.8.1 Textual Evidence

Sympathy by Charles Mackay

I lay in sorrow, deep distressed;
My grief a proud man heard;
His looks were cold, he gave me gold,
But not a kindly word.

My sorrow passed-I paid him back
The gold he gave to me;
Then stood erect and spoke my thanks
And blessed his charity.
I lay in want, in grief and pain;
A poor man passed my way;
He bound my head, He gave me bread,
He watched me day and night.

How shall I pay him back again
For all he did to me ?
Oh, gold is great, but greater far
Is heavenly sympathy.

1. The reader can tell from the third stanza that the poet is

Ⓐ caring for a patient with a head injury.
Ⓑ wanting company.
Ⓒ watched and fed night and day by a poor man.
Ⓓ greedy.

2. According to the poet, what did he feel was most important?

Ⓐ giving away food
Ⓑ blessing charity
Ⓒ sympathy
Ⓓ gold

3. What does the first stanza tell us about the poet?

Ⓐ The poet experienced an event that made him deeply sorrowful.
Ⓑ The poet wrote this poem when he was a proud man.
Ⓒ The poet wrote this poem when he was in need of money.
Ⓓ The poet was friends with a proud man.

Patrick couldn't believe it. The most important day of his life so far; the day he had been waiting for had finally arrived! He was so excited to show the coaches how hard he had been working on his pitching. He just knew he would make the team this year. Looking at the clock, Patrick realized he was running late. "Bye, Mom," he yelled as he scrambled out of the house. Backing down the driveway, he saw his mom run out of the house, and it looked like she was trying to get his attention. He didn't have time to wait, so he drove off.

Although the school was only five minutes away, the drive felt like an eternity. Two red lights later, Patrick screeched into the parking lot, slammed the car into park, and ran around to the trunk to get his bat bag. It wasn't there. Every piece of equipment he needed to prove himself to the coaches this year was in that bag.

4. Part A

What was Patrick's mom likely trying to tell Patrick?

Ⓐ "Don't drive too fast!"
Ⓑ "Don't be late for tryouts!"
Ⓒ "Be careful driving!"
Ⓓ He forgot his bat bag!

4. Part B

The reader can tell from the story that Patrick _____.

Ⓐ had tried out for the team before and not made it.
Ⓑ was a fast runner.
Ⓒ was not at all ready for tryouts.
Ⓓ was not excited to try out for the team.

RL.8.1 Inferences

Haley was putting the finishing touches on her famous apple pie when the phone rang. She dashed to answer it. After all, this might be the call that she had been waiting for. Even though her hands were still covered in flour, she grabbed the phone before it could ring a second time.

"Hello. You've reached the Williams residence," she said, trying to make her voice sound calm and collected.

"Is this Haley Williams?" asked the voice on the other end of the line.

"Yes, it is. How may I help you?" Haley replied.

"Ms. Haley Williams, we are proud to announce that you are a finalist in the National Pie Competition. The championship round will be held next weekend in Tampa, Florida. You and your family are invited to join us. Good luck!"

"Why, thank you very much," Haley said graciously. "I am looking forward to it." After hanging up, Haley took a deep breath and let out an ear-piercing scream of excitement. She jumped up and down and ran around the kitchen with glee. In the pandemonium, her apple pie was knocked off the counter and landed on the floor, where her two puppies immediately began to gobble it down. Haley just laughed at the mess. As she cleaned the floor, she began to think very carefully about her plan for the upcoming week.

With the big competition only one week away, Haley decided that she better make three pies every day. This practice would allow her to experiment with the crust, the filling, and the baking time. She wanted to do everything she possibly could to ensure that her pie was a winner.

Her friend, Max, who was thrilled to find out that Haley was a finalist, offered his kitchen for practice. Haley thanked him. She knew that cooking in an unfamiliar kitchen would be excellent practice for the competition.

Haley worked hard all week, doing nothing but baking pies. Not every pie turned out well. Some had a soggy crust or burned a little on the top. Haley threw out the bad pies and carefully wrapped the successful pies, and delivered them to her neighbors and friends. They were all delighted by the surprise and wished Haley good luck at the competition.

The day before the competition, Haley packed up all of the things she would need. She brought her favorite rolling pin for good luck. When she arrived in Tampa, Florida, she went straight to her hotel and got a good night's rest. The competition started early the next morning, and Haley wanted to be ready.

The day of the competition seemed to fly by in one big blur. Haley was one of twelve finalists. Each finalist had their own countertop on which to prepare their pie and their own oven in which to bake it. Once everyone was set up at their station, the master of ceremonies officially started the clock, and everyone got to work. Every contestant had 90 minutes to prepare and bake their pies. Haley mixed and rolled out her pie dough. Then she peeled and sliced her apples, laying them carefully inside the crust. She seasoned the pie with cinnamon and sugar and laid strips of dough on top. She brushed the pie crust with butter and glanced at the clock. She was right on schedule; her pie took 45 minutes to bake, and there were just 47 minutes left on the clock.

Haley opened the oven door, but she immediately noticed that something was wrong.

She didn't feel a rush of dry heat in her face, and she realized that she had forgotten to preheat the oven. The oven wasn't hot, and it would take several minutes to reach the correct temperature.

Haley felt her heart sink into her stomach. How could she forget such an important step? In all her practice, she had never forgotten to preheat the oven. Haley figured that she didn't stand a chance of winning, but she refused to give up. She put her pie in the oven and set the oven to the correct temperature.

With 30 seconds left in the competition, Haley removed her pie from the oven. It wasn't golden on the top, but it looked like it was cooked through. Haley sighed, disappointed that she had blown her chances at winning. But she delivered her pie to the judges and hoped for the best.

After tasting each pie and deliberating for hours, the judges handed the results to the master of ceremonies. "In third place….Haley Williams!" the voice boomed over the loudspeaker. Haley couldn't believe her ears. She walked to the front of the room to accept her trophy with a smile on her face. She knew that if it hadn't been for her mistake, she might have won the grand prize.

But, she just hugged her trophy, congratulated herself on her accomplishment, and promised herself that she would do better next year.

After reading the story, enter the details in the map below. This will help you to answer the questions with ease.

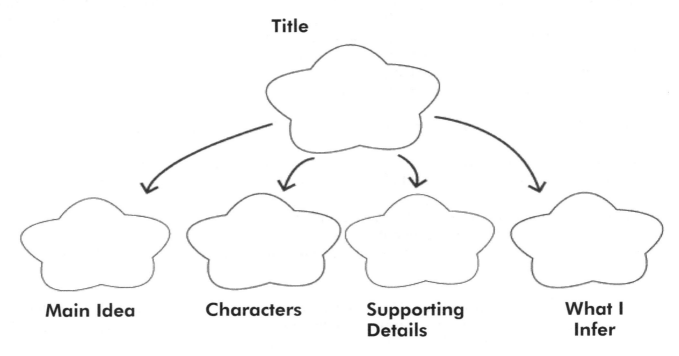

Title

Main Idea   **Characters**   **Supporting Details**   **What I Infer**

1. What can be inferred from Haley's reaction to the phone ringing?

Ⓐ   She isn't concerned about the phone call.
Ⓑ   She doesn't think washing her hands is important.
Ⓒ   She is expecting an important phone call.
Ⓓ   She is enjoying talking to her family.

Henry sat eagerly in the waiting area of the airport. Over the last year, he'd been putting away a little money each month into what he called his "vacation fund." He bought travel books and researched all of the sites he wanted to see. Now all he had to do was wait until his flight was called.

2. What can you infer about Henry's trip?

Ⓐ   It was a spur of the moment idea.
Ⓑ   It is something he has looked forward to for a long time.
Ⓒ   It is to a place he's been before.
Ⓓ   It is an exotic location.

She pulled hard at the doorknob. The door was difficult to budge. Finally inside, she brushed aside the cobwebs, leaving footprints in the dust on the floor.

3. What can be inferred from this description?

Ⓐ The place she is entering hasn't been used for a long time.
Ⓑ The house she is entering is a new structure.
Ⓒ The door was locked.
Ⓓ She has just bought the house and is preparing to move in.

Justin had Mark's deep brown eyes and his button nose. At only three years old, he already showed signs of Mark's sense of humor and optimism. Mark was proud that Justin had inherited some of his traits.

4. Based on the description above, one could infer that Justin _____

Select the correct answer choice from the 4 options given below and fill in the blank.

Ⓐ is friends with Mark
Ⓑ is Mark's brother
Ⓒ is Mark's son
Ⓓ is Mark's sister

RL.8.2 Theme

The Fox and the Cat-An Aesop's Fable

A Fox was boasting to a Cat of its clever devices for escaping its enemies.

"I have a whole bag of tricks," he said, "which contains a hundred ways of escaping my enemies."

"I have only one," said the Cat, "but I can generally manage with that."

Just at that moment, they heard the cry of a pack of hounds coming towards them, and the Cat immediately scampered up a tree and hid in the boughs.

"This is my plan," said the Cat. "What are you going to do?"

The Fox thought first of one way, then of another, and while he was debating, the hounds came nearer and nearer, and at last, the Fox in his confusion was caught up by the hounds and soon killed by the huntsmen. The Cat, who had been looking on, said, "Better one safe way than a hundred on which you cannot reckon."

After reading the story, enter the details in the map below. This will help you to answer the questions with ease.

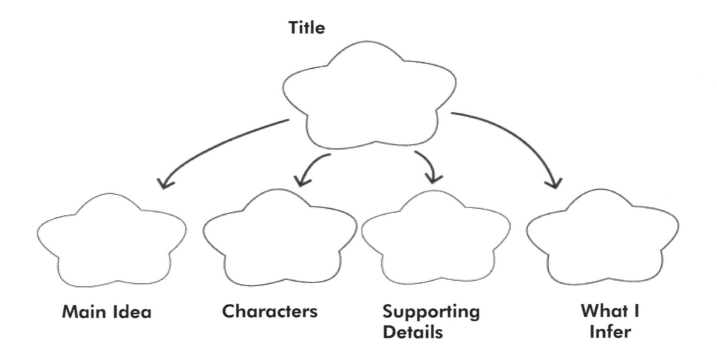

Title

Main Idea   **Characters**   **Supporting Details**   **What I Infer**

1. What is the theme of this story?

Ⓐ It is good to make friends with strangers.
Ⓑ It is better to be a cat than a fox.
Ⓒ Having one solid plan is better than having many possible ones.
Ⓓ Foxes are not as smart as cats.

The Ungrateful Son
by Jacob and Wilhelm Grimm

Once, a man was sitting with his wife before their front door. They had a roasted chicken, which they were about to eat together. Then the man saw that his aged father was approaching, and he hastily took the chicken and hid it, for he did not want to share it with him. The old man came, had a drink, and went away. Now the son wanted to put the roasted chicken back onto the table, but when he reached for it, it had turned into a large toad, which jumped into his face and sat there and never went away again. If anyone tried to remove it, it looked venomously at him as though it would jump into his face so that no one dared to touch it. And the ungrateful son was forced to feed the toad every day, or else it would eat from his face. And thus, he went to and fro in the world without rest.

2. Part A
What is the theme of this story?

Ⓐ The theme of the story is to always share what you have to share.
Ⓑ The theme of the story is to not be afraid of toads because they can keep you from saving someone's life.
Ⓒ The theme of the story is that you should always feed yourself first, and then you will be strong enough to help others.
Ⓓ The theme of the story is that you should always share your chicken with your parents.

2. Part B
The theme of The Ungrateful Son is implied because _____.

Ⓐ It is indirectly stated, and the reader has to determine the theme through the actions of the characters.
Ⓑ It is explicitly stated, and the reader does not have to guess at all.
Ⓒ It is obvious and doesn't require much thought.
Ⓓ none of the above

The Laundry

Charlie's parents always assigned him chores around the house. They would often ask him to trim the lawn, wash the dishes, and feed the dog. However, his chores never included laundry. He relied on his mother to wash his clothes for him. Charlie was an outstanding student and was recently accepted to a top college. The college he planned to attend was in New York City. Charlie was nervous about leaving Texas, where he grew up, and being so far away from his family, but he knew that the college in New York was the perfect fit for him. Before he left, his mother decided that she had better show him how to wash his own clothes because she wouldn't be there to do it for him anymore. She showed Charlie how to sort his clothes into two piles: whites and colors.

Then she showed him how much soap to use and told him when to use hot or warm water and when to use cold water. Next, she explained the different settings on the dryer and told him to be careful not to dry certain items on high heat. Charlie didn't pay much attention. He didn't see what could happen or what was so complicated about washing clothes. He planned on packing mostly t-shirts and jeans and figured that it would be hard to mess up something so simple. When Charlie arrived at school, and he was completely overwhelmed with all of the exciting things to do and new people to meet. He was also careful to dedicate plenty of time to his schoolwork because he wanted to impress his professors and earn good grades. One morning Charlie woke up and found that he had no clean clothes to wear. His schedule had been so packed with activities and studying that he had managed to get through the first month of school without doing any laundry. That night, Charlie piled his soiled clothes into a large basket and headed to his dormitory's laundry room. He shoved all of his clothes into a washer, poured in the soap, and pressed the start. Half an hour later, he opened the washer and started moving the clothes into the dryer. It was then that he realized that he had skipped one very significant step. All of his white t-shirts and socks had turned pink. He had forgotten to sort his colors from his whites. Charlie had received a bright red t-shirt with his new school's logo across the front. The red dye had bled in the wash, turning all of his white clothes pink. Charlie was unhappy about his destroyed wardrobe, but he figured that there was absolutely nothing to do except to put the clothes in the dryer and hope for the best. So he transferred the clothes to a dryer and set the heat to high. After all, he was anxious to get back upstairs to his studies. An hour later, Charlie removed his clothes from the dryer and headed straight back to his dorm room. The following morning, he reached for one of his favorite t-shirts. It was slightly pink now, but he didn't have enough money to replace all of his newly pink clothes. He would have to wear them pink or not. As he pulled the shirt over his head, he noticed that it seemed tight. He looked at himself in the mirror.

The shirt had shrunk in the dryer. It looked like he had tried to squeeze into his little sister's pink t-shirt. All Charlie could do was laugh. He called his mom and asked her to repeat her laundry instructions again.

This time, Charlie took notes.

3. What is the theme of this story?

Circle the correct answer choice.

Ⓐ Pay close attention when you are learning something new.
Ⓑ Always ask for help.
Ⓒ Learn how to do your laundry when you are young.
Ⓓ Always have your parents do your laundry.

The Fox and the Crow-An Aesop's Fable

A Fox once saw a Crow fly off with a piece of cheese in its beak and settle on a branch of a tree. "That's for me, as I am a Fox," said Master Reynard, and he walked up to the foot of the tree. "Good-day, Mistress Crow," he cried. "How well you are looking today: how glossy your feathers; how bright your eye. I feel sure your voice must surpass that of other birds, just as your figure does; let me hear but one song from you that I may greet you as the Queen of Birds." The Crow lifted up her head and began to caw her best, but the moment she opened her mouth, the piece of cheese fell to the ground, only to be snapped up by Master Fox. "That will do," said he. "That was all I wanted. In exchange for your cheese, I will give you a piece of advice for the future."

4. What is the theme of this story?

Ⓐ Help out your friends.
Ⓑ Don't trust flatterers.
Ⓒ Sometimes, a song is necessary.
Ⓓ You should never have to work for food.

RL.8.2 Objective Summary

The Ungrateful Son- by Jacob and Wilhelm Grimm

Once, a man was sitting with his wife before their front door. They had a roasted chicken, which they were about to eat together. Then the man saw that his aged father was approaching, and he hastily took the chicken and hid it, for he did not want to share it with him. The old man came, had a drink, and went away. Now the son wanted to put the roasted chicken back onto the table, but when he reached for it, it had turned into a large toad, which jumped into his face and sat there and never went away again. If anyone tried to remove it, it looked venomously at him as though it would jump into his face so that no one dared to touch it. And the ungrateful son was forced to feed the toad every day, or else it would eat from his face. And thus, he went to and fro in the world without rest.

After reading the story, enter the details in the map below. This will help you to answer the questions with ease.

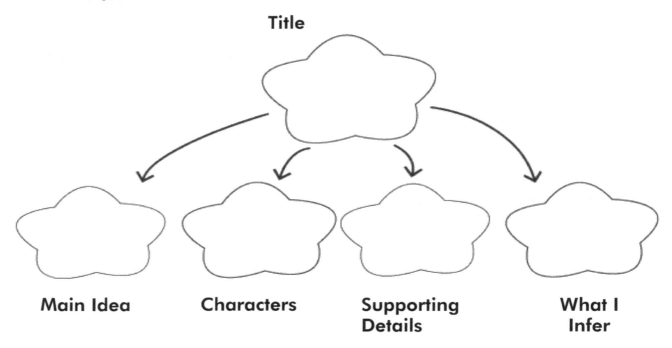

Title

Main Idea   Characters   Supporting Details   What I Infer

1. What is the best summary of this passage?

The Ant and the Grasshopper-An Aesop's Fable

In a field, one summer's day, a grasshopper was hopping about, chirping and singing to its heart's content. A group of ants walked by, grunting as they struggled to carry plump kernels of corn. "Where are you going with those heavy things?" asked the grasshopper. Without stopping, the first ant replied, "To our anthill. This is the third kernel I've delivered today."

"Why not come and sing with me," teased the grasshopper, "instead of working so hard?"

"We are helping to store food for the winter," said the ant, "and think you should do the same."

"Winter is far away, and it is a glorious day to play," sang the grasshopper. But the ants went on their way and continued their hard work.

The weather soon turned cold. All the food lying in the field was covered with a thick white blanket of snow that even the grasshopper could not dig through.

Soon the grasshopper found itself dying of hunger. He staggered to the ants' hill and saw them handing out corn from the stores they had collected in the summer. He begged them for something to eat.

"What!" cried the Ants in surprise, "haven't you stored anything away for the winter? What in the world were you doing all last summer?"

"I didn't have time to store any food," complained the grasshopper; "I was so busy playing music that before I knew it, the summer was gone."

The ants shook their heads in disgust, turned their backs on the grasshopper, and went on with their work.

2. What is the best summary for the story?

When I was finished with my doctor's appointment, I made my way to the lobby. My mom was going to pick me up, but knowing how she was always late, I realized I had some time to spare. I took a seat in the lobby and smiled politely at the three elderly people sitting near me. There were two women and an old man. Then I dug into my backpack for my library book.

Soon, one of the women and the man left. It was just the beautiful gray-haired woman in the lobby and me.

3. What is the best summary for the story?

The Emperor Penguin is the only penguin species that breeds during the Antarctic winter. It treks 31–75 miles over the ice to breeding colonies, which may include thousands of penguins. The female lays a single egg, which is then incubated by the male while the female returns to the sea to feed; parents subsequently take turns foraging at sea and caring for their chick in the colony. The average lifespan of the Emperor Penguin is 20 years, although observations suggest that some Emperor Penguins may live to 50 years of age.

4. Read the summary below. Select the answer below that best explains why the summary provided cannot be considered a proper objective summary.

Breeding during the winter in Antarctica is specific to the Emperor Penguin. The Emperor Penguin travels far; they will travel anywhere from 31 – 75 miles in the freezing cold to meet many other penguins for breeding. This is known as a breeding colony, and a colony can have thousands of penguins. The father penguins sit on the eggs while the mothers go and hunt for food at sea. After the chick is born, the mother and father take turns taking care of the baby and going off to feed. Emperor Penguins, on average, live to be about 20 years old, but some have been known to live up to 50 years.

Ⓐ   The summary is incorrect because it includes the writer's opinion.
Ⓑ   The summary is perfect and should be considered proper.
Ⓒ   The summary is incorrect because it is not a summary; it is a paraphrase of the passage.
Ⓓ   The summary is incorrect because it is not accurate.

RL.8.2 Plot

Walk-A-Thon

It was clear there weren't enough funds for the 8th-grade graduation ceremony at the end of the year. Big deal – why should I care? I was on the student council, but I never cared about graduation ceremonies.

It costs about $5,000.00 for the rent, equipment, insurance, and all the other incidentals that pile up when planning a large event. Principal Dorsey told us that he didn't have the money this year. He said that if we wanted to keep the graduation tradition going, we would have to raise the money ourselves. "I'm sure we can live without the ceremony, but it would be nice to have," he told us. Then he left the meeting.

Immediately, Katrina Reynolds shot her hand in the air. She's not very popular, and I always feel kind of sorry for her. "We have to do this, you guys," Katrina gushed. "There is no way we are going to be the only class ever not to have a graduation ceremony."

Then, of course, Abbie Morelle, who was President, shot her hand in the air. I'd been on Student Council for two years, and as far as I could remember, Abbie had never let Katrina say anything without disagreeing with it. "It's very late in the year," Abbie said. "And we already have the Band Land Dance scheduled, which we don't have enough money for. We can't raise $7,000 in, like, two months."

Paulie Roman, who was treasurer, said, "According to my records, it would be more like $7,012, although we can't be certain of the precise cost of unspecified expenses related to the ceremony."

I didn't care. To me, 8th grade is pure misery, no matter what you do. If you have a great graduation ceremony at the end of it, that's like saying, "We had such a great time in all of our boring classes and with all of the bullies every day. Let's have a party to celebrate them!" But I was all for a fundraiser if it would get Abbie Morelle off Katrina's back.

I said, "Let's do a walk-a-thon. We could raise a lot of money that way."

"Walk-a-thons are stupid," Abbie said.

Paulie Roman asked, "How much money could we raise with a walk-a-thon?"

I said, "When we did a walk-a-thon for cancer research in elementary school, we raised $4,000. This school is twice as big, and people can walk farther."

"Yeah," Abbie said, "but that was for cancer. Why would anyone give us money for a graduation ceremony? Plus, someone has to organize it, and it's complicated."

That got me mad enough that I had to say, "It's not that complicated. I'll do it."

What was I thinking? I spent the next month doing almost nothing except organizing that walk-a-thon. I hate walk-a-thons, and I hate talking to people about money. I ended up doing way more than I ever wanted to.

Within the first two weeks, I could see that we weren't going to get enough. It was because we weren't raising money for something important, like cancer. So I started telling people that the money would also go for cancer research. Then, when I saw how many people were ready to give more, I just told them it was all for cancer research. I got hundreds of parents signed up, and I got businesses to donate food and decorations.

Abbie was completely jealous.

The walk-a-thon was almost a success, too. But the day before, Principal Dorsey called me into his office. He wanted to know if it was true that I had been telling people that the money would go to cancer research because he had understood the money was going or our 8th-grade graduation party. I didn't answer. He said that he was going to call some of the people who pledged money to ask them if I had said anything about cancer.

"It was the only way I could raise enough money!" I answered back, knowing the lie had caught up with me.

"Well, it was the wrong thing to do." Principal Dorsey replied. "Now, you are going to have to contact every person who donated and let them know the truth. You also may not have enough money for a graduation party now."

I knew I should never have volunteered to lead this.

1. What is the major type of conflict in this story?

Ⓐ external: man vs fate
Ⓑ external: man vs man
Ⓒ internal: man vs himself
Ⓓ external: man vs nature

2. What is the conflict in this story?

Ⓐ there is not enough money for an 8th-grade graduation party
Ⓑ who is most popular
Ⓒ who will organize the walk-a-thon
Ⓓ whether or not to have graduation

3. What is the exposition in this story?

Ⓐ I didn't care. To me, 8th-grade is pure misery, no matter what you do. If you have a great graduation ceremony at the end of it, that's like saying, "We had such a great time in all of our boring classes and with all of the bullies every day. Let's have a party to celebrate them!" But I was all for a fundraiser if it would get Abbie Morelle off Katrina's back.

Ⓑ He wanted to know if it was true that I had been telling people that the money would go to cancer research, because he had understood the money was going or our 8th-grade graduation party.

Ⓒ Principal Dorsey told us that he didn't have the money this year. He said that if we wanted to keep the graduation tradition going, and we would have to raise the money ourselves.

Ⓓ It was clear there weren't enough funds for the 8th-grade graduation ceremony at the end of the year. Big deal – why should I care? I was on the Student Council, but I never cared about graduation ceremonies.

4. Part A
What is the climax of this story?

Ⓐ when the narrator volunteers to be in charge of the walk-a-thon
Ⓑ when the narrator lies about why she is collecting the money
Ⓒ when the principal calls the narrator to the office and the narrator confesses to lying about the cause
Ⓓ when the narrator makes Abbie jealous

4. Part B
What is the most important event in the falling action of this story?

Ⓐ when the narrator learns she must contact all the donors
Ⓑ when the narrator learns there will be no graduation party
Ⓒ when the narrator makes Abbie jealous
Ⓓ when the narrator organizes the walk-a-thon

RL.8.2 Setting

Megan couldn't believe her luck. She had been standing in line with her best friend, Jessica, for thirty minutes. Their excitement was mounting as they neared the front of the line for the famed Greased Lightning roller coaster. Just as they took their seats, the clouds opened up. Soaking wet and disappointed, the girls followed the directions of the ride employees and took shelter under the nearby canopies.

1. Which of the following does not help the reader to gain a sense of the setting?

Ⓐ the time of day
Ⓑ the weather
Ⓒ the time of year
Ⓓ the mood of the main character

It had been a year since Lauren had seen Bailey. Bailey's family had moved to Qatar, leaving Lauren to face the world without her best friend. Anxiously, Lauren waited at the arrival gate, hoping to glimpse a peek at her childhood friend. She knew after eleven hours in the air, and Bailey would be exhausted; but, she could hardly wait to catch up. Moments later, the doors to the gate flung open, and there was her best friend, Bailey.

Once home, the hours passed like minutes as the girls laughed and giggled, sharing moments from the last year. It felt as if they had never been apart. But Lauren felt like Bailey was holding something back.

2. What is the primary setting for this passage?

Ⓐ an airport
Ⓑ Lauren's house
Ⓒ Bailey's house
Ⓓ There is not enough information to determine the setting.

From **Chapter 5 of Peter Pan** by J.M. Barrie

"He lay at his ease in a rough chariot drawn and propelled by his men, and instead of a right hand, he had the iron hook with which ever and anon he encouraged them to increase their pace. As dogs, this terrible man treated and addressed them, and as dogs, they obeyed him. In-person he was ca-daverous [dead looking] and [dark faced], and his hair was dressed in long curls, which at a little distance looked like black candles, and gave a singularly threatening expression to his handsome countenance. His eyes were of the blue of the forget-me-not, and of a profound melancholy, save when he was plunging his hook into you, at which time two red spots appeared in them and lit them up horribly. A man of indomitable courage, it was said that the only thing he shied at was the sight of his own blood, which was thick and of an unusual color. But undoubtedly the grimmest part of him was his iron claw."

3. What is the setting of the above paragraph from the excerpt?

University of California Berkeley scientists confirmed that a cluster of fossilized bones found in Silicon Valley is likely the remains of a mammoth. The giant beast would have roamed the area between 10,000 and 40,000 years ago. A pair of elephant-like tusks, a huge pelvic bone, and the animal's rib cage were found by an amateur naturalist who was walking a dog along a canal near San Jose's Guadalupe River. It could be the remains of a Columbian mammoth, according to paleontologists who expect to study the site.

4. What is the setting of this article?

Ⓐ Columbia
Ⓑ University of California Berkeley
Ⓒ a canal near the Guadalupe River in the Silicon Valley
Ⓓ Berkeley

RL.8.2 Character

1. What is a static character?

   (A)   a character that changes during the course of the story
   (B)   a character that does not change during the course of the story
   (C)   a character with a smaller role that is not important to the development of the story
   (D)   a character with a large role that is not vital to the development of the story

2. What is a dynamic character?

   (A)   a character that changes during the course of the story
   (B)   a character that does not change during the course of the story
   (C)   a character with a smaller role that is not important to the development of the story
   (D)   a character with a large role that is not vital to the development of the story

Walk-A-Thon

It was clear there weren't enough funds for the 8th-grade graduation ceremony at the end of the year. Big deal – why should I care? I was on the student council, but I never cared about graduation ceremonies.

It costs about $5,000.00 for the rent, equipment, insurance, and all the other incidentals that pile up when planning a large event. Principal Dorsey told us that he didn't have the money this year. He said that if we wanted to keep the graduation tradition going, we would have to raise the money ourselves. "I'm sure we can live without the ceremony, but it would be nice to have," he told us. Then he left the meeting.

Immediately, Katrina Reynolds shot her hand in the air. She's not very popular, and I always feel kind of sorry for her. "We have to do this, you guys," Katrina gushed. "There is no way we are going to be the only class ever not to have a graduation ceremony."

Then, of course, Abbie Morelle, who was President, shot her hand in the air. I'd been on Student Council for two years, and as far as I could remember, Abbie had never let Katrina say anything without disagreeing with it. "It's very late in the year," Abbie said. "And we already have the Band Land Dance scheduled, which we don't have enough money for. We can't raise $7,000 in, like, two months."

Paulie Roman, who was treasurer, said, "According to my records, it would be more like $7,012, al-though we can't be certain of the precise cost of unspecified expenses related to the ceremony."

I didn't care. To me, 8th grade is pure misery, no matter what you do. If you have a great graduation ceremony at the end of it, that's like saying, "We had such a great time in all of our boring classes

and with all of the bullies every day. Let's have a party to celebrate them!" But I was all for a fundraiser if it would get Abbie Morelle off Katrina's back.

I said, "Let's do a walk-a-thon. We could raise a lot of money that way."

"Walk-a-thons are stupid," Abbie said.

Paulie Roman asked, "How much money could we raise with a walk-a-thon?"

I said, "When we did a walk-a-thon for cancer research in elementary school, we raised $4,000. This school is twice as big, and people can walk farther."

"Yeah," Abbie said, "but that was for cancer. Why would anyone give us money for a graduation ceremony? Plus, someone has to organize it, and it's complicated."

That got me mad enough that I had to say, "It's not that complicated. I'll do it."

What was I thinking? I spent the next month doing almost nothing except organizing that walk-a-thon. I hate walk-a-thons, and I hate talking to people about money. I ended up doing way more than I ever wanted to.

Within the first two weeks, I could see that we weren't going to get enough. It was because we weren't raising money for something important, like cancer. So I started telling people that the money would also go for cancer research. Then, when I saw how many people were ready to give more, I just told them it was all for cancer research. I got hundreds of parents signed up, and I got businesses to donate food and decorations.

Abbie was completely jealous.

The walk-a-thon was almost a success, too. But the day before, Principal Dorsey called me into his office. He wanted to know if it was true that I had been telling people that the money would go to cancer research because he had understood the money was going or our 8th-grade graduation party. I didn't answer. He said that he was going to call some of the people who pledged money to ask them if I had said anything about cancer.

"It was the only way I could raise enough money!" I answered back, knowing the lie had caught up with me.

"Well, it was the wrong thing to do." Principal Dorsey replied. "Now, you are going to have to contact every person who donated and let them know the truth. You also may not have enough money for a graduation party now."

I knew I should never have volunteered to lead this.

3. **What sort of character is the narrator?**

   Ⓐ major
   Ⓑ minor
   Ⓒ middle
   Ⓓ weak

4. **Part A**
   What sort of character is Principal Dorsey?

   Ⓐ major
   Ⓑ minor
   Ⓒ middle
   Ⓓ weak

4. **Part B**
   What type of character is Abbie Morelle?

   Ⓐ round
   Ⓑ flat
   Ⓒ bumpy
   Ⓓ none of the above

RL.8.3 Analyzing Literature

Casey Jones-A Tennessee Legend-retold by S.E. Schlosser

Casey Jones, that heroic railroad engineer of the Cannonball, was known as the man who always brought the train in on time. He would blow the whistle, so it started off soft but would increase to a wail louder than a banshee before dying off. Got so as people would recognize that whistle and know when Casey was driving past.

April 29, 1900, Casey brought the Cannonball into Memphis dead on time. As he was leaving, he found out one of the other engineers was sick and unable to make his run. So Casey volunteered to help out his friend. He pulled the train out of the station about eleven p.m., an hour and thirty-five minutes late. Casey was determined to make up the time. As soon as he could, he highballed out of Memphis (highballing means to go very fast and take a lot of risks to get where you are headed) and started making up for the lost time.

About four a.m., when he had nearly made up all the time on the run, Casey rounded a corner near Vaughan, Mississippi, and saw a stalled freight train on the track. He shouted for his fireman to jump. The fireman made it out alive, but Casey Jones died in the wreck, one hand on the brake and one on the whistle chord.

1. Which of the statements below best describes Casey Jones?

Ⓐ   He was a large, friendly man known to most as the Cannonball.
Ⓑ   He was a courageous and punctual man.
Ⓒ   He was so concerned about being punctual, and he was not careful when driving.
Ⓓ   none of the above

2. What do Casey's actions in the last paragraph reveal about him?

Ⓐ   He wasn't very smart because he didn't jump off the train in time.
Ⓑ   He did not care for his firemen.
Ⓒ   Up to his very last act, he was courageous.
Ⓓ   none of the above

The Grasshopper and the Ants-Aesop's Fable

In a field, one summer's day, a grasshopper was hopping about, chirping and singing to its heart's content. A group of ants walked by, grunting as they struggled to carry plump kernels of corn. "Where are you going with those heavy things?" asked the grasshopper. Without stopping, the first ant replied, "To our anthill. This is the third kernel I've delivered today."

"Why not come and sing with me," teased the grasshopper, "instead of working so hard?"

"We are helping to store food for the winter," said the ant, "and think you should do the same."

"Winter is far away, and it is a glorious day to play," sang the grasshopper. But the ants went on their way and continued their hard work.

The weather soon turned cold. All the food lying in the field was covered with a thick white blanket of snow that even the grasshopper could not dig through.

Soon the grasshopper found itself dying of hunger. He staggered to the ants' hill and saw them handing out corn from the stores they had collected in the summer. He begged them for something to eat. "What!" cried the Ants in surprise, "haven't you stored anything away for the winter? What in the world were you doing all last summer?"

"I didn't have time to store any food," complained the grasshopper; "I was so busy playing music that before I knew it, the summer was gone."

The ants shook their heads in disgust, turned their backs on the grasshopper, and went on with their work.

3. What does the response of the first ant to the grasshopper reveal for readers?

   Ⓐ He is taking his work seriously.
   Ⓑ He doesn't like grasshoppers.
   Ⓒ He likes to work alone.
   Ⓓ He has just started working and doesn't want to be bothered.

The Laundry

Charlie's parents always assigned him chores around the house. They would often ask him to trim the lawn, wash the dishes, and feed the dog. However, his chores never included laundry. He relied on his mother to wash his clothes for him. Charlie was an outstanding student and was recently accepted to a top college. The college he planned to attend was in New York City. Charlie was nervous about leaving Texas, where he grew up, and being so far away from his family; but, he knew that the college in New York was the perfect fit for him. Before he left, his mother decided that she had better show him how to wash his own clothes because she wouldn't be there to do it for him anymore. She showed Charlie how to sort his clothes into two piles: whites and colors.

Then she showed him how much soap to use and told him when to use hot or warm water and when to use cold water. Next, she explained the different settings on the dryer and told him to be careful not to dry certain items on high heat. Charlie didn't pay much attention. He didn't see what could happen or what was so complicated about washing clothes. He planned on packing mostly t-shirts and jeans and figured that it would be hard to mess up something so simple.

When Charlie arrived at school, and he was completely overwhelmed with all of the exciting things to do and new people to meet. He was also careful to dedicate plenty of time to his schoolwork because he wanted to impress his professors and earn good grades. One morning Charlie woke up and found that he had no clean clothes to wear. His schedule had been so packed with activities and studying that he had managed to get through the first month of school without doing any laundry. That night, Charlie piled his soiled clothes into a large basket and headed to his dormitory's laundry room. He shoved all of his clothes into a washer, poured in the soap, and pressed the start. Half an hour later, he opened the washer and started moving the clothes into the dryer. It was then that he realized that he had skipped one very significant step. All of his white t-shirts and socks had turned pink. He had forgotten to sort his colors from his whites. Charlie had received a bright red t-shirt with his new school's logo across the front. The red dye had bled in the wash, turning all of his white clothes pink. Charlie was unhappy about his destroyed wardrobe, but he figured that there was absolutely nothing to do except to put the clothes in the dryer and hope for the best. So he transferred the clothes to a dryer and set the heat to high. After all, he was anxious to get back upstairs to his studies. An hour later, Charlie removed his clothes from the dryer and headed straight back to his dorm room. The following morning, he reached for one of his favorite t-shirts. It was slightly pink now, but he didn't have enough money to replace all of his newly pink clothes. He would have to wear them pink or not. As he pulled the shirt over his head, he noticed that it seemed tight. He looked at himself in the mirror.

The shirt had shrunk in the dryer. It looked like he had tried to squeeze into his little sister's pink t-shirt. All Charlie could do was laugh. He called his mom and asked her to repeat her laundry instructions again.

This time, Charlie took notes.

4. Part A
What does this excerpt reveal about Charlie?

Ⓐ   Charlie did not ask his mother for help with his clothes.
Ⓑ   Charlie did not listen carefully to his mother's instructions on how to wash his clothes.
Ⓒ   Charlie tried to enjoy doing his laundry.
Ⓓ   Charlie is so eager to get his homework completed on time that he forgets the laundry instructions.

4. Part B
After Charlie had a mishap with his laundry, he laughed. What does this reveal about Charlie's character?

Ⓐ   Charlie is the kind of person who realizes what's done is done; all he can do is try again.
Ⓑ   Charlie is the kind of person who laughs wildly when he isn't sure how to react to stressful situations.
Ⓒ   Charlie is the kind of person who laughs at the misfortune of others.
Ⓓ   Charlie is the kind of person who laughs when he isn't sure what to do.

RL.8.4 Meaning and Tone

Excerpt from Because of Winn-Dixie-by Kate DiCamillo

The Open Arms had mice. They were there from when it was a Pick-It-Quick, and there were lots of good things to eat in the building, and when the Pick-It-Quick became the Open Arms Baptist Church of Naomi, the mice stayed around to eat all the leftover crumbs from the potluck suppers. The preacher kept on saying he was going to have to do something about them, but he never did. Because the truth is, he couldn't stand the thought of hurting anything, even a mouse.

Well, Winn-Dixie saw that mouse, and he was up and after him. One minute, everything was quiet and serious, and the preacher was going on and on and on, and the next minute, Winn-Dixie looked like a furry bullet, shooting across the building, chasing that mouse. He was barking, and his feet were skidding all over the polished Pick-It-Quick floor, and people were clapping and hollering and pointing. They really went wild when Winn-Dixie actually caught the mouse.

1. What is the tone in this excerpt?

- Ⓐ romantic
- Ⓑ unemotional
- Ⓒ enthusiastic
- Ⓓ morose

Excerpt from "The Story of the Wild Huntsman" by Heinrich Hoffmann

This is the Wild Huntsman that shoots the hares
With the grass-green coat he always wears:
With game-bag, powder-horn and gun,
He's going out to have some fun.
He finds it hard, without a pair
Of spectacles, to shoot the hare:
He put his spectacles upon his nose, and said,
"Now I will shoot the hares, and kill them dead."
The hare sits snug in leaves and grass
And laughs to see the green man pass.

2. What is the tone of this excerpt?

- Ⓐ joyous
- Ⓑ formal
- Ⓒ serious
- Ⓓ comical

3. In the excerpt, "The Story of the Wild Huntsman," what does "snug" most likely mean?

    Ⓐ   seaworthiness
    Ⓑ   fitting closely
    Ⓒ   privacy
    Ⓓ   humorous

4. In the excerpt, "The Story of the Wild Huntsman," what does "spectacles" most likely means?

    Ⓐ   something unusual
    Ⓑ   something one would be curious about
    Ⓒ   dramatic display
    Ⓓ   glasses

RL.8.5 Compare and Contrast

1. When you are contrasting two things, what are you looking for?

Ⓐ similarities
Ⓑ differences
Ⓒ similarities and differences
Ⓓ none of the above

2. In a Venn diagram, where does the "common" information belong?

Ⓐ in the middle
Ⓑ on the right
Ⓒ on the left
Ⓓ no where

3. Which of the following group of signal words would you most likely find in a paper contrasting two things?

Ⓐ in addition, finally, above all
Ⓑ meanwhile, coupled with, for instance
Ⓒ likewise, as well, the same as
Ⓓ although, however, contrary to

Henry Wordsworth Longfellow was an American poet who lived from 1807 to 1882. Longfellow was born and raised in the region of Portland, Maine. Longfellow was enrolled in dame school at the age of only three. By age six, when he entered Portland Academy, he was able to read and write quite well. He graduated from Bowdoin College in Brunswick, Maine, in 1822. At Bowdoin, he met Nathaniel Hawthorne, who became his lifelong friend. After several journeys overseas, Longfellow settled for the last forty-five years of his life in Cambridge, Massachusetts. Longfellow was one of the five members of the group known as the Fireside Poets. During his years at the college, he wrote textbooks in French, Italian, and Spanish and a travel book, Outre-mer: A Pilgrimage Beyond the Sea Longfellow was such an admired figure in the United States during his life that his 70th birthday in 1877 took on the air of a national holiday, with parades, speeches, and the reading of his poetry. He had become one of the first American celebrities. His work was immensely popular during his time and is still today, although some modern critics consider him too sentimental. His poetry is based on familiar and easily understood themes with simple, clear, and flowing language. His poetry created an audience in America and contributed to creating American mythology.

Ralph Waldo Emerson was an American essayist, poet, and leader of the trancendentalist movement in the early 19th century. He was born and brought up in Boston, Massachusetts. Emerson lost his father at the age of 8 and was subsequently sent to Boston Latin School at the age of 9. He went to Harvard College at the age of 14 and graduated in 1821. Emerson made his living as a schoolmaster and then went to Harvard Divinity School and emerged as a Unitarian Minister in 1829. A dispute with church officials over the administration of the Communion service and misgivings about public prayer led to his resignation in 1832. In the 1840's Emerson was hospitable to Nathanial Hawthorne and his family, influencing Hawthorne during his three joyous years with Emerson. Emerson was noted as being a very abstract and difficult writer who nevertheless drew large crowds for his speeches. The heart of Emerson's writing were his direct observations in his hournals, which he started keeping as a teenager at Harvard. Emerson has written a lot of essays on, History, Self-reliance, love, friendship, heroism etc... He died in 1882 and is buried in the sleepy hollow Cemetery, Concord, Massachusetts. His house, which he bought in 1835 in Concord, Massachusetts, is now open to the public as the Ralph Waldo Emerson house.

4. According to the above passages, what is common between the above writers?

Ⓐ   Both the writers were born in America.
Ⓑ   Both the writers lived at the same time (19th Century).
Ⓒ   Both the writers were associated with Nathaniel Hawthorne.
Ⓓ   All of the above.

RL.8.6 Producing Suspense and Humor

It was a cold and windy evening. The clouds had a haunting presence in the sky. Cindy walked briskly down the street, conscious of the quiet around her. As she approached her front door, she noticed something wasn't right. There was a light on inside, and she thought she could hear someone running down the stairs. Her husband, however, wasn't due home for a couple of hours.

1. This description builds a sense of _____.

Ⓐ irony
Ⓑ suspense
Ⓒ humor
Ⓓ confusion

In the story Romeo and Juliet by William Shakespeare, Romeo commits suicide because he thinks that Juliet is dead. However, the reader knows that she is just in a deep sleep because she took a potion that made her appear dead.

2. What type of irony does Shakespeare use?

Ⓐ dramatic irony
Ⓑ verbal irony
Ⓒ situational irony
Ⓓ none of the above

A man wakes up early to wash his car before a trip to the park to watch a baseball game. After the game, he realizes that he parked under a tree filled with birds, and now his car is covered in white splattered patches. The man said with a loud sigh, "Gee, I sure am glad I woke up early to wash my car."

3. What type of irony does the author use?

Ⓐ dramatic irony
Ⓑ verbal irony
Ⓒ situational irony
Ⓓ none of the above

The Tempest, Act III, Scene II [Be not afeard]

William Shakespeare, 1564 - 1616

Caliban speaks to Stephano and Trinculo.

Be not afeard; the isle is full of noises,
Sounds and sweet airs, that give delight, and hurt not.
Sometimes a thousand twangling instruments
Will hum about mine ears; and sometime voices,
That, if I then had waked after long sleep,
Will make me sleep again: and then, in dreaming,
The clouds methought would open, and show riches
Ready to drop upon me; that, when I waked,
I cried to dream again.

4. Describe what not to be afraid of? Write your answer in the box below.

___

RL.8.7 Media and Literature

The Lake Isle of Innisfree

I will arise and go now, and go to Innisfree,
And a small cabin build there, of clay and wattles made:
Nine bean-rows will I have there, a hive for the honey-bee;
And live alone in the bee-loud glade.
And I shall have some peace there, for peace comes dropping slow,
Dropping from the veils of the morning to where the cricket sings;
There midnight's all a glimmer, and noon a purple glow,
And evening full of the linnet's wings.
I will arise and go now, for always night and day
I hear lake water lapping with low sounds by the shore;
While I stand on the roadway, or on the pavements grey,
I hear it in the deep heart's core.
W. B. Yeats

About the poet:
William Butler Yeats was an Irish poet and a dramatist. He was one of the foremost figures of 20th century literature and was the driving force behind the Irish literary revival. Together with Lady Gregory and Edward Martin, Yeats founded the Abbey Theater. He served as its chief during its early years and was a pillar of the Irish literary establishment in his later years.

The above well-known poem explores the poet's longing for the peace and tranquility of Innisfree, a place where he spent a lot of time as a boy. This poem is a lyric.

image obtained from freephotobank.com

1. **Which medium of publication, the poem or the picture, gives you a better visualization of the lake?**

   Ⓐ the picture
   Ⓑ the poem
   Ⓒ neither
   Ⓓ both

2. **Which medium of publication, the poem or the picture, appeals to more than one of the five senses?**

   Ⓐ the picture
   Ⓑ the poem
   Ⓒ neither
   Ⓓ both

3. **Part A**
   Which medium of publication, the poem or the picture, is the best to visualize the lake and its surroundings?

   Ⓐ the picture
   Ⓑ the poem
   Ⓒ neither
   Ⓓ both

3. **Part B**
   Which medium of publication, the poem or the picture, would be best to use on a travel brochure to attract people to the lake?

   Ⓐ the picture
   Ⓑ the poem
   Ⓒ neither
   Ⓓ both

Casey Jones-A Tennessee Legend-retold by S.E. Schlosser

Casey Jones, that heroic railroad engineer of the Cannonball, was known as the man who always brought the train in on time. He would blow the whistle, so it started off soft but would increase to a wail louder than a banshee before dying off. It got so as people would recognize that whistle and know when Casey was driving past.

April 29, 1900, Casey brought the Cannonball into Memphis dead on time. As he was leaving, he found out one of the other engineers was sick and unable to make his run. So Casey volunteered to help out his friend. He pulled the train out of the station about eleven p.m., an hour and thirty-five minutes late. Casey was determined to make up the time. As soon as he could, he highballed out of Memphis (highballing means to go very fast and take a lot of risks to get where you are headed) and started making up for the lost time.

About four a.m., when he had nearly made up all the time on the run, Casey rounded a corner near Vaughn, Mississippi, and saw a stalled freight train on the track. He shouted for his fireman to jump. The fireman made it out alive, but Casey Jones died in the wreck, one hand on the brake and one on the whistle chord.

4. What medium of publication would be best to use if you wanted to make it possible for people to see Casey Jones operating the train?

Ⓐ a video
Ⓑ digital text
Ⓒ a traditional book
Ⓓ none of the above

RL.8.9 Modern Fictions and Traditional Stories

There is a boy who has three brothers. His bike is broken, so he goes to borrow one of his brother's. His oldest brother's bike is way too big. His younger brother's bike still has training wheels on it and is too small. His second oldest brother's bike works perfectly, though, and that is the one he borrowed.

1. What traditional story does this remind you of?

Ⓐ "Little Red Riding Hood"
Ⓑ The Story of "Goldilocks and the Three Bears"
Ⓒ "Rumpelstiltskin"
Ⓓ "Snow White and the Seven Dwarfs"

You read a story about a young girl who battles against all the odds to overcome the hardships of homelessness and discrimination to go to Harvard and become extremely successful.

2. What is a popular motif in this story?

Ⓐ good vs. evil
Ⓑ a test of courage
Ⓒ children who are heroes
Ⓓ true love

3. In the classic fairy tale "Cinderella," what do the characters of Cinderella and the stepmother stand for?

Ⓐ fun vs. boring
Ⓑ good vs. evil
Ⓒ young vs. old
Ⓓ traditional vs. non-traditional

4. "When someone declares an event to be a modern-day Cinderella story they mean
_____.

   Fill in the blank after selecting the correct answer choice from the 4 options given below."

   Ⓐ someone poor or common becomes successful
   Ⓑ someone has evil step-sisters
   Ⓒ someone rides a carriage
   Ⓓ someone is the most beautiful in her family

Answer Key and Detailed Explanations

Reading: Literature

RL.8.1 Textual Evidence

Question No.	Answer	Detailed Explanations
1.	C	Answer choice C is correct. Lines 3 and 4 in the third stanza provide the text evidence. There is no text evidence supporting answer choices A, B or D.
2.	C	Answer choice C is correct and directly stated in the last two lines of the poem. Answer choice D is incorrect. While the poet does recognize gold is good, he states sympathy is greater. Answer choices A and B do not provide evidence to support the question.
3.	A	Answer choice A is correct because the first line of the poem indicates the poet's sorrow. The other answer choices are incorrect as there is no evidence in the first stanza to support them.
4. Part A	D	Answer choice D is correct. Patrick was in such a hurry he did not check to see if his bag was in the trunk of his car. His mom realized he had left it and ran out to remind him. There is no evidence to support answer choices A, B, or C.
4. Part B	A	Answer choice A is correct. The word this in the sentence, "he just knew he would make the team this year" indicates that Patrick has tried out before and not made the team. There is no evidence to support answer choices B, C, or D.

RL.8.1 Inferences

Question No.	Answer	Detailed Explanations
1.	C	Answer choice C is correct. Haley is so eager to answer the phone, she doesn't even take a moment to wash the flour off her hands. Answer choice A is incorrect because it is not supported in the text. Answer choice B is incorrect because it is likely Haley doesn't wash her hands because of her eagerness to answer the phone call.
2.	B	Answer choice B is correct because Henry has been saving his money for a year and did research on his destination. Answer choice A is incorrect because Henry has been saving his money, so the trip was planned. Answer choice C is incorrect because Henry did research on his destination. Answer choice D cannot be inferred from the text.
3.	A	Answer choice A is correct. The door was hard to open because it hadn't been opened in quite some time. Additionally, there were cobwebs in the room and dust on the floor meaning no one had entered the room in a long time. Answer choice B is incorrect because it is unlikely a new building would have cobwebs and a layer of dust in it. Answer choice C is incorrect because she was able to get in. The door was not locked, just stuck. Answer choice D is incorrect because there is no evidence to support the inference.
4.	C	Answer choice C is correct. Mark has inherited some of the traits and characteristics of his father. Answer choices A, B and D cannot be inferred from the text.

RL.8.2 Theme

Question No.	Answer	Detailed Explanations
1.	C	Answer choice C is correct. The Fox bragged to the Cat that he had several ways of escaping his enemy. The Cat only knew one way to escape and used it. The Fox wasted too much time trying to decide which method of escape he should choose and ended up getting caught. Answer choices A, B, and D are not themes of this story.
2. Part A	A	Answer choice A is correct. Had the man offered to share his chicken, it would not have turned into a toad forever requiring attention. Answer choices B, C and D are incorrect because none of them are themes of this story.
2. Part B	A	Answer choice A is correct. The theme is implicitly stated. That is, the reader must use the actions of the man, hiding the roasted chicken so he doesn't have to share, to determine the theme of the text. Answer choices B, C and D are incorrect because they are not reasonable.
3.	A	Answer choice A is correct. Charlie learned that he should have listened to his mom when she was giving him instructions on doing the laundry. In this example, the reader thinks about what Charlie learned and then restates the lesson so that it applies universally - pay close attention when you are learning something new. This applies to both Charlie and the world (universal). Answer choices B, C, and D are not themes of this story.
4.	B	Answer choice B is correct. The Crow learns that she should not be so trusting of someone who lavishes her with compliments. Considered universally, the theme then becomes don't be trusting of flatterers. Answer choices A, C and D are not themes of this story.

RL.8.2 Objective Summary

Question No.	Answer	Detailed Explanations
1.	-	A man hid his dinner from his father so he didn't have to share it. Because the man was greedy, the chicken turned into a toad and he was forced to care for it for the rest of his life.
2.	--	During the summer, the ants stowed food so they would not go hungry during the winter. The grasshopper spent his summer playing music, so when winter came, he had nothing to eat.
3.	--	After a doctor's appointment, the narrator waits in the lobby for his mother to pick him up. At the end, only he and a woman remain in the lobby.
4.	C	Answer choice C is correct. The summary provided simply paraphrases, or mixes up the words, the passage. Summaries must be original and not paraphrased. Answer choice A is incorrect because the summary is objective. Answer choice B is incorrect because the summary is not perfect. Answer choice D is incorrect because the information contained within the summary is correct. Remember, though, a summary should not be paraphrased.

RL.8.2 Plot

Question No.	Answer	Detailed Explanations
1.	A	Answer choice A is correct. The conflict is that there is not enough money for a graduation party. This conflict is man vs fate because the students had no direct control. There are other conflicts in the story, but the major conflict is the lack of money. Answer choices B, C, and D are incorrect.
2.	A	Answer choice A is correct. The conflict in the story is that there is not enough money for 8th-grade graduation party. It is worth noting that the reader learns of the conflict in the introduction of the story. Answer choices B, C, and D are incorrect.
3.	D	Answer choice D is correct. The introduction or exposition is where the reader is introduced to the character, setting, and conflict. The exposition occurs at the beginning of the story. Answer choices A, B, and C are incorrect as they are not part of the introduction or exposition of the story.
4. Part A	C	Answer choice C is correct. The climax is the turning point, and the narrator's confession is the turning point. The reader doesn't know if the principal will let the students keep the money or make them return it. Answer choices A, B, and D are not the climax of the story.
4. Part B	A	Answer choice A is correct. The most important event in the falling action is when the narrator learns she must contact all the donors and tell them the truth about what their donations were funding. Answer choices B, C, and D are not part of the falling action of this story.

RL.8.2 Setting

Question No.	Answer	Detailed Explanations
1.	D	Answer choice D is correct. The mood of the main character, also known as the protagonist, cannot help the reader to determine the setting. However, the time of day, weather, and time of year all help to contribute to the setting.
2.	A	Answer choice A is correct. Clues to help the reader understand the setting is in an airport include Lauren waiting at the arrival gate and the reference to eleven hours in the air. Answer choices B, C and D are incorrect.
3.	--	There is not enough information to determine the setting of this excerpt as it is a description of a character.
4.	C	Answer choice C is correct. The setting is where the fossils were found which is by a canal near the Guadalupe River in the Silicon Valley. Answer choice A is incorrect as the setting is not in Columbia. Answer choice B is incorrect. The scientists working with the fossils are from The University of California Berkeley. Answer choice D is incorrect because the reader is able to determine the setting.

RL.8.2 Character

Question No.	Answer	Detailed Explanations
1.	B	Answer choice B is correct. A static character does not experience any sort of change during the course of a story. Answer choices A, C, and D are incorrect.
2.	A	Answer choice A is correct. A dynamic character is one who changes during the course of the story due to the events that occur in the story. Answer choices B, C, and D are incorrect.
3.	A	Answer choice A is the correct answer. The narrator is the major character in the story because she is the most important character and propels the story forward. The narrator is also the protagonist. Answer choices B, C and D are incorrect.
4. Part A	B	Answer choice B is correct. Principal Dorsey is a minor character; however his character is important to the development of the story. Answer choices A, C, and D are incorrect.
4. Part B	B	Answer choice B is correct. The character of Abbie Morelle is flat because the reader does not learn much about her. The author did not provide much information about Abbie, so the reader only gets to see one side of her. Answer choice A is incorrect because the reader does not learn much about the character. Answer choice C is incorrect.

RL.8.3 Analyzing Literature

Question No.	Answer	Detailed Explanations
1.	B	Answer choice B is correct. Casey Jones was a courageous man who was concerned about getting his train to its destination on time. Casey did not expect to see another train stalled on the tracks; therefore, he was not prepared to stop. As his last act of courage, Casey warned anyone nearby of impending doom by blowing the whistle and trying to stop the train. Answer choices A, C, and D are incorrect.
2.	C	Answer choice C is correct. As the train rounded the corner, Casey could see disaster ahead and warned the firemen. This is the act of a courageous man. Answer choices A, B, and D are incorrect.
3.	A	Answer choice A is correct. The ant is too busy to stop working and instead carries the kernel while explaining what he is doing to the grasshopper. The ant knows that he must continue with the work in order to be prepared for the upcoming winter. Answer choices B, C, and D are incorrect.
4. Part A	B	Answer choice B is correct. Charlie shoves all his laundry into the machine at once which was not part of the laundry instructions his mom gave him. Answer choice A, C, and D could be true, but the reader must consider only the excerpt provided.
4. Part B	A	Answer choice A is correct. Because of Charlie's reaction to his shrunken, miscolored clothes, it is evident he doesn't overreact when faced with obstacles but works to find solutions. Answer choices B, C, and D are incorrect.

RL.8.4 Meaning and Tone

Question No.	Answer	Detailed Explanations
1.	C	Answer choice C is correct. The tone of the excerpt is enthusiastic. DiCamillo wants the reader to feel excited while reading this passage. Answer choices A, B, and D are incorrect.
2.	D	Answer choice D is correct. The tone is comical as Hoffmann describes the bumbling huntsman and hiding hare. Answer choices A, B, and C are incorrect.
3.	B	Answer choice B is correct. The hare is hiding from the huntsman in the leaves and grass. He is not noticed as the huntsman walks past because he is snug or fitting closely in the leaves and grass. Answer choices A, C, and D are incorrect.
4.	D	Answer choice D is correct. In this excerpt, "spectacles" most closely means glasses. The huntsman realizes he cannot see to hunt without his spectacles or glasses. Humorously, even with his spectacles, or glasses, perched upon his nose, he still does not see the hare hiding. Answer choices A, B, and C are incorrect.

RL.8.5 Compare and Contrast

Question No.	Answer	Detailed Explanations
1.	B	The correct answer is B. When you are contrasting, you are looking for differences. When you are looking at two pieces of text, if you are asked about contrasts, you are being asked to tell the difference between the two pieces of text. Answer choices A, C, and D are incorrect.
2.	A	The correct answer is A. Common information in a Venn diagram goes in the middle where the two circles intersect. Contrasting information goes in the outer portions of the circle. Answer choices B, C, and D are incorrect.
3.	D	Answer choice D is correct. A paper or article that is contrasting two things will likely use signal words such as although, however, contrary to, unlike, and unless. These are not the only signal words, but they are quite common. Answer choices A, B, and C are incorrect.
4.	D	Answer choice D is correct. According to the passages, Longfellow and Emerson were born in America, lived in the 19th century, and were familiar with Nathaniel Hawthorne.

RL.8.6 Producing Suspense and Humor

Question No.	Answer	Detailed Explanations
1.	B	Answer choice B is correct. The author builds suspense by setting up a mood of apprehension and including foreshadowing. Answer choices A, C, and D are incorrect.
2.	A	Answer choice A is correct. Dramatic irony is used because the reader knows something that the character of Romeo does not know. Believing his beloved is dead, he kills himself. Answer choices B, C, and D are incorrect.
3.	B	Answer choice B is correct. Verbal irony is used because the man says he is happy he woke up early to wash his car, but in reality his efforts were futile since his car is now dirty. He did not sincerely mean what he said. Answer choices A, C, and D are incorrect.
4.	Noise	This scene describes the type of noises not to be afraid of.

RL.8.7 Media and Literature

Question No.	Answer	Detailed Explanations
1.	A	Answer choice A is correct because the image is only of the lake. The poem speaks of the lake, but it speaks more of the boy's memories associated with the lake.
2.	B	Answer choice B is correct because the poem talks about both sounds and sights.
3. Part A	B	Answer choice B is correct because the question asks about both the lake and its surroundings. The image only shows the lake.
3. Part B	A	Answer choice A is correct because the poem is about the author's personal cabin at the lake; therefore, it's not a travel destination while the image is of the entire lake and therefore open to the public.
4.	A	Answer choice A is correct because a video allows people to see a visualization.

RL.8.9 Modern Fictions and Traditional Stories

Question No.	Answer	Detailed Explanations
1.	B	Answer choice B is correct. This story is a loose retelling of the fairy tale, "Goldilocks and the Three Bears" by Robert Southey. Traditional stories are often times retold into modern versions, thus the story lives on and is more applicable to modern times.
2.	B	Answer choice B is correct. The popular motif in this short story is a test of courage (character's actions). This is a loose adaptation of the classic fairy tale "Cinderella".
3.	B	Answer choice B is correct. Remember that fairy tales always include a good character and an evil character. In "Cinderella," Cinderella is the good character and her step-mother is evil, thus their characters represent good vs. evil.
4.	A	Answer choice A is correct. Modern day Cinderella are people who overcome odds and become successful.

Reading: Informational Text

The objective of the Reading Informational Text standards is to ensure that the student is able to read and comprehend informational texts (history/social studies, science, and technical texts) related to the grade. We encourage the student to go through the resources available online on Lumos EdSearch to gain an in depth understanding of the related concepts. A small mind map is provided after each passage or text in which the student can enter the details as understood from the literary text. Doing this will help the student to refer to key points that help in answering the questions with ease.

RI.8.1 Making Inferences Based on Textual Evidence

Stephen and Joseph Montgolfier were papermakers, but they had been interested in flying for many years. One night, in 1782, Joseph noticed something that gave him an idea. He was sitting in front of the fire when he saw some small pieces of scorched paper being carried up the chimney.

Soon afterward, the brothers conducted an experiment. They lit a fire under a small silk bag, which was open at the bottom; at once, the bag rose to the ceiling. After this, Stephen and Joseph conducted many more experiments, both indoors and in the open air. Eventually, they built a huge balloon of linen and paper. On June 5th, 1783, they launched their balloon in the village of Annonay.

1. **What evidence in the passage shows that the Montgolfier brothers discovered how to make a hot air balloon?**

   Ⓐ "He was sitting in front of the fire when he saw some small pieces of scorched paper being carried up the chimney."
   Ⓑ "Eventually, they built a huge balloon of linen and paper. On June 5th, 1783, they launched their balloon in the village of Annonay."
   Ⓒ "After this, Stephen and Joseph conducted many more experiments, both indoors and in the open air."
   Ⓓ none of the above

2. **What evidence in the text shows that the Montgolfier brothers launched the first successful hot air balloon?**

   Ⓐ "He was sitting in front of the fire when he saw some small pieces of scorched paper being carried up the chimney."
   Ⓑ "Eventually, they built a huge balloon of linen and paper. On June 5th, 1783, they launched their balloon in the village of Annonay."
   Ⓒ "After this, Stephen and Joseph conducted many more experiments, both indoors and in the open air."
   Ⓓ none of the above

3. **What evidence in the text could lead you to infer that the Montgolfier brothers' experienced some trial and error before successfully launching a hot air balloon?**

Ⓐ "He was sitting in front of the fire when he saw some small pieces of scorched paper being carried up the chimney."
Ⓑ "Eventually, they built a huge balloon of linen and paper. On June 5th, 1783, they launched their balloon in the village of Annonay."
Ⓒ "After this, Stephen and Joseph conducted many more experiments, both indoors and in the open air."
Ⓓ none of the above

4.Part A
Which specific detail in the above passage describes the first experiment the brothers did?

Ⓐ Stephen and Joseph Montgolfier were papermakers, but they had been interested in flying for many years.
Ⓑ He was sitting in front of the fire when he saw some small pieces of scorched paper being carried up the chimney.
Ⓒ After this, Stephen and Joseph conducted many more experiments, both indoors and in the open air.
Ⓓ They lit a fire under a small silk bag, which was open at the bottom; at once, the bag rose to the ceiling.

4.Part B
The reader can tell from the article that Joseph Montgolfier was very observant because

Ⓐ He created a balloon from paper and linen.
Ⓑ He noticed the small pieces of burnt paper being carried up the chimney.
Ⓒ He found the best location to launch the balloon.
Ⓓ He was interested in flying..

RI.8.2 Central Idea

The Emperor Penguin is the only penguin species that breeds during the Antarctic winter. It treks 31–75 miles over the ice to breeding colonies, which may include thousands of penguins. The female lays a single egg, which is then incubated by the male while the female returns to the sea to feed; parents subsequently take turns foraging at sea and caring for their chick in the colony. The average lifespan of the Empire Penguin is 20 years, although observations suggest that some Emperor Penguins may live to 50 years of age.

1.   **What is the central idea of this passage?**

Ⓐ The movie, Happy Feet was inspired by Emperor Penguins.
Ⓑ The male Emperor Penguin sits on the egg while the mother hunts for food.
Ⓒ Female Emperor penguins lay their eggs in the Antarctic and both male and female take turns caring for the egg until it hatches.
Ⓓ Emperor Penguins live over 50 years.

Archaeology is the study of past human life and culture through systematically examining and interpreting the material remains left behind. These material remains include archaeological sites (e.g. settlements, building features, graves), as well as cultural materials or artifacts such as tools and pottery. Through the interpretation and classification of archaeological materials, archaeologists work to understand past human behavior. In some countries, archaeology is often historical or art historical, with a strong emphasis on Culture history, archaeological sites, and artifacts such as art objects. In the New World, archaeology can be either a part of history and classical studies or anthropology.

The exact origins of archaeology as a discipline are uncertain. Excavations of ancient monuments and the collection of antiquities have been taking place for thousands of years. It was only in the 19th century, however, that the systematic study of the past through its physical remains underwent professionalization, which meant it began to be carried out in a manner recognizable to modern students of archaeology.

2. **What is the central idea of this passage?**

Ⓐ the study of the origin of archaeology
Ⓑ the study of archaeology
Ⓒ the study of modern archaeology and anthropology
Ⓓ the study of the human past

3. What does the passage suggest about archaeologists?

Ⓐ They study past human life and culture by examining materials left by early humans.
Ⓑ They study humans and their interactions with their surroundings.
Ⓒ They study humans and their families by looking at the things they left behind.
Ⓓ They study art history.

Marathon

Training for a marathon takes hard work and perseverance. It is not something you can do on the spur of the moment. Preparing for a marathon takes months, particularly if you have never run a marathon before. The official distance of a full marathon is 26.2 miles. In 2005, the average time to complete a marathon in the United States was 4 hours 32 minutes 8 seconds for men and 5 hours 6 minutes 8 seconds for women.

Most people who run marathons are not trying to win. Many runners try to beat their own best time. Some compare their time to other runners in the same gender and age group. Some people set time-oriented goals, such as finishing under four hours, while others try to complete the race without slowing to a walk. Many beginners simply hope to finish the marathon.

Trainers recommend that beginners maintain a consistent running schedule for six weeks prior to even starting a marathon training program. The purpose of this is to allow the body to adapt to the various physical demands of long-distance running. First-time marathon runners should train by running four days a week for at least four months, increasing distance by no more than ten percent weekly. As race day approaches, runners should taper their runs, reducing the strain on their bodies and resting before the marathon. It is important not to overexert yourself during training because that can lead to a lot of injuries. Most common injuries are spraining of the knees and ankles. These sprains can hinder the training.

Before the race, it is important to stretch in order to keep muscles limber. Staying hydrated is also important, but there is a danger in drinking too much water. If a runner drinks too much water, they may experience a dangerous condition called hyponatremia, a drop of sodium levels in the blood. So only drink water when you are thirsty. During the race, trainers recommend maintaining a steady pace. It is normal to feel sore after a marathon. Light exercise will help sore muscles heal faster.

Some people run marathons in pairs or groups. Training for and running a marathon with another person or group of people can make the experience more enjoyable and more rewarding. A running partner might be just the motivation you need to show up for an early morning run instead of rolling over to hit the snooze button. And, when you cross the finish line together, you can share the satisfaction of reaching your common goal.

Usually, thousands of people sign up and run a marathon. Most people finish the race. The thrill of running a marathon for the first time is unbelievable. The training sessions are harder if you have never run before. But it is unbelievable what ones' body can do when one puts his/her mind to it. Having a good coach to support you makes all the difference in training for a marathon.

The daily runs are very important. Strength training and core training are also very important.

The health benefits you gain from training are tremendous. Your core muscles grow stronger, and you will have tighter thighs and gluts. Your heart will be much stronger, and you can maintain lower cholesterol and blood sugar levels. Overall, you will look better and become healthier.
Nothing can explain how people feel when they reach that finish line at the end of the race. All the hard work and months of training feel worthwhile. The feeling of accomplishing something great overtakes you. It is great to run a marathon, but it is even greater to finish it.

4. Part A
How would you go about determining the central idea of this passage?

- Ⓐ read the title
- Ⓑ read the passage
- Ⓒ pay attention to the details
- Ⓓ all of the above

4. Part B
What is the central idea of the passage?

- Ⓐ the health benefits of the running of a marathon
- Ⓑ how to run a marathon
- Ⓒ what it takes to prepare for and run a marathon
- Ⓓ none of the above

Name: _____ Date: _____

RI.8.3 Connections and Distinctions

Cooking quinoa is much like cooking rice. Depending on the sort of quinoa you purchase, you may have to rinse the seed-like spores before cooking. Be sure to check the label. Boil two cups of water, vegetable stock, chicken broth or other liquid of your choice. Add one cup of raw (rinsed if necessary) quinoa and simmer for about twenty minutes. It doesn't take long for quinoa to cook up moist and tender.

1. What is one distinction that the passage reminds you to take?

Ⓐ The type of quinoa you buy will determine if you have to rinse.
Ⓑ There are different types of quinoa that taste differently.
Ⓒ Always feel the quinoa before buying it.
Ⓓ The type of liquid to use is your choice.

Marathon

Training for a marathon takes hard work and perseverance. It is not something you can do on the spur of the moment. Preparing for a marathon takes months, particularly if you have never run a marathon before. The official distance of a full marathon is 26.2 miles. In 2005, the average time to complete a marathon in the United States was 4 hours 32 minutes 8 seconds for men and 5 hours 6 minutes 8 seconds for women.

Most people who run marathons are not trying to win. Many runners try to beat their own best time. Some compare their time to other runners in the same gender and age group. Some people set time-oriented goals, such as finishing under four hours, while others try to complete the race without slowing to a walk. Many beginners simply hope to finish the marathon.

Trainers recommend that beginners maintain a consistent running schedule for six weeks prior to even starting a marathon training program. The purpose of this is to allow the body to adapt to the various physical demands of long-distance running. First-time marathon runners should train by running four days a week for at least four months, increasing distance by no more than ten percent weekly. As race day approaches, runners should taper their runs, reducing the strain on their bodies and resting before the marathon. It is important not to overexert yourself during training because that can lead to a lot of injuries. Most common injuries are spraining of the knees and ankles. These sprains can hinder the training.

Before the race, it is important to stretch in order to keep muscles limber. Staying hydrated is also important, but there is a danger in drinking too much water. If a runner drinks too much water, they may experience a dangerous condition called hyponatremia, a drop of sodium levels in the blood. So only drink water when you are thirsty. During the race, trainers recommend maintaining a steady pace. It is normal to feel sore after a marathon. Light exercise will help sore muscles heal faster.

Some people run marathons in pairs or groups. Training for and running a marathon with another person or group of people can make the experience more enjoyable and more rewarding. A running partner might be just the motivation you need to show up for an early morning run instead of rolling over to hit the snooze button. And, when you cross the finish line together, you can share the satisfaction of reaching your common goal.

Usually, thousands of people sign up and run a Marathon. Most people finish the race. The thrill of running a marathon for the first time is unbelievable. The training sessions are harder if you have never run before. But it is unbelievable what ones' body can do when one puts their mind to it. Having a good coach to support you makes all the difference in training for a marathon.

The daily runs are very important. Strength training and core training are also very important.

The health benefits you gain from training are tremendous. Your core muscles grow stronger, and you will have tighter thighs and gluts. Your heart will be much stronger, and you can maintain lower cholesterol and blood sugar levels. Overall, you will look better and become healthier.

Nothing can explain how people feel when they reach that finish line at the end of the race. All the hard work and months of training feel worthwhile. The feeling of accomplishing something great overtakes you. It is great to run a marathon, but it is even greater to finish it.

2. Part A
How is a marathon competition different than most competitions?

Ⓐ Runners compete against themselves to beat past times.
Ⓑ Runners do not compete against each other.
Ⓒ Runners set their own personal records.
Ⓓ all of the above

2. Part B
What makes marathon running similar to other competitive sports?

Ⓐ health benefits
Ⓑ trophies
Ⓒ winning
Ⓓ numbers of people

3. What does it mean to make a distinction?

- Ⓐ to find a similarity
- Ⓑ to find a difference
- Ⓒ to draw a conclusion
- Ⓓ to point out a fact

4. What does it mean to make a connection?

- Ⓐ to find a similarity
- Ⓑ to find a difference
- Ⓒ to draw a conclusion
- Ⓓ to point out a fact

RI.8.4 Determining Meaning of Words

Marathon

Training for a marathon takes hard work and perseverance. It is not something you can do on the spur of the moment. Preparing for a marathon takes months, particularly if you have never run a marathon before. The official distance of a full marathon is 26.2 miles. In 2005, the average time to complete a marathon in the United States was 4 hours 32 minutes 8 seconds for men and 5 hours 6 minutes 8 seconds for women.

Most people who run marathons are not trying to win. Many runners try to beat their own best time. Some compare their time to other runners in the same gender and age group. Some people set time-oriented goals, such as finishing under four hours, while others try to complete the race without slowing to a walk. Many beginners simply hope to finish the marathon.

Trainers recommend that beginners maintain a consistent running schedule for six weeks prior to even starting a marathon training program. The purpose of this is to allow the body to adapt to the various physical demands of long-distance running. First-time marathon runners should train by running four days a week for at least four months, increasing distance by no more than ten percent weekly. As race day approaches, runners should taper their runs, reducing the strain on their bodies and resting before the marathon. It is important not to overexert yourself during training because that can lead to a lot of injuries. Most common injuries are spraining of the knees and ankles. These sprains can hinder the training.

Before the race, it is important to stretch in order to keep muscles limber. Staying hydrated is also important, but there is a danger in drinking too much water. If a runner drinks too much water, they may experience a dangerous condition called hyponatremia, a drop of sodium levels in the blood. So only drink water when you are thirsty. During the race, trainers recommend maintaining a steady pace. It is normal to feel sore after a marathon. Light exercise will help sore muscles heal faster.

Some people run marathons in pairs or groups. Training for and running a marathon with another person or group of people can make the experience more enjoyable and more rewarding. A running partner might be just the motivation you need to show up for an early morning run instead of rolling over to hit the snooze button. And, when you cross the finish line together, you can share the satisfaction of reaching your common goal.

Usually, thousands of people sign up and run a Marathon. Most people finish the race. The thrill of running a marathon for the first time is unbelievable. The training sessions are harder if you have never run before. But it is unbelievable what ones' body can do when one puts their mind to it. Having a good coach to support you makes all the difference in training for a marathon.

The daily runs are very important. Strength training and core training are also very important.

The health benefits you gain from training are tremendous. Your core muscles grow stronger, and you will have tighter thighs and gluts. Your heart will be much stronger, and you can maintain lower cholesterol and blood sugar levels. Overall, you will look better and become healthier.

Nothing can explain how people feel when they reach that finish line at the end of the race. All the hard work and months of training feel worthwhile. The feeling of accomplishing something great overtakes you. It is great to run a marathon, but it is even greater to finish it.

"Nothing can explain how people feel when they reach that finish line at the end of the race. All the hard work and months of training feel worthwhile."

1. Part A
What does the phrase "overexert" (third paragraph) mean?

Ⓐ go over the amount of time you need to run
Ⓑ go over the distance you need to run
Ⓒ do more than your body can handle
Ⓓ drink too much water

1. Part B
What does the phrase "spur of the moment" (first paragraph) mean?

Ⓐ at the moment, without thinking
Ⓑ at the last minute
Ⓒ on a horse wearing spurs
Ⓓ taking time to train

2. How does the phrase "spur of the moment" add to the tone of the passage?

Ⓐ It creates a humorous tone, so the readers laugh and enjoy the piece.
Ⓑ It creates a serious tone necessary to show how hard running a marathon is.
Ⓒ It creates a factual tone so readers can study before training.
Ⓓ It creates a reminder of how important training is.

3. What is connotation?

Ⓐ a dictionary definition
Ⓑ what a word means based on its context in a story
Ⓒ a word with multiple meanings
Ⓓ an opinion based on the fact

4. What is denotation?

Ⓐ a dictionary definition
Ⓑ what a word means based on its context in a story
Ⓒ a word that has a meaning that has changed over time
Ⓓ an opinion based on the fact

RI.8.5 Analyzing Structures in Text

Stephen and Joseph Montgolfier were papermakers, but they had been interested in flying for many years. One night, in 1782, Joseph noticed something that gave him an idea. He was sitting in front of the fire when he saw some small pieces of scorched paper being carried up the chimney.

Soon afterward, the brothers conducted an experiment. They lit a fire under a small silk bag, which was open at the bottom; at once, the bag rose to the ceiling. After this, Stephen and Joseph conducted many more experiments, both indoors and in the open air. Eventually, they built a huge balloon of linen and paper. On June 5th, 1783, they launched their balloon in the village of Annonay.

1. What would change this passage into an essay?

Ⓐ adding an introductory paragraph and a conclusion
Ⓑ adding more details to the experiments
Ⓒ adding nothing, it is already an essay
Ⓓ rewriting it as a personal narrative

2. What type of text structure is used in this passage?

Ⓐ sequence
Ⓑ compare/contrast
Ⓒ cause/effect
Ⓓ description

The Emperor Penguin is the only penguin species that breeds during the Antarctic winter. It treks 31–75 miles over the ice to breeding colonies, which may include thousands of penguins. The female lays a single egg, which is then incubated by the male while the female returns to the sea to feed; parents subsequently take turns foraging at sea and caring for their chick in the colony. The average lifespan of the Empire Penguin is 20 years, although observations suggest that some Emperor Penguins may live to 50 years of age.

3. What type of text structure is used in the passage above?

Ⓐ sequence
Ⓑ compare/contrast
Ⓒ description
Ⓓ cause/effect

The Eagle	First Flight
Far from the habitations of humans and their petty quarrels, there once lived on top of a rugged hill, an old eagle. When the fragrant morning breeze blew through his nest, the eagle would shake his feathers and spread out his wings. When the sun rose high, and the world below engaged itself in its unceasing fight for survival, the eagle would take off from the hilltop and circle majestically over the valley and its dwellers, the fields, and the running brooks. If he saw something worthwhile, such as a hare or a rat, a pigeon or a chick, he would swoop down on it like lightning, fetch it to his nest, and devour it. He would then inspect the surroundings once again.	The young seagull was alone on his ledge. His two brothers and his sister had already flown away the day before. He had afraid to fly with them. Somehow, when he had taken a little run forward to the brink of the ledge and attempted to flap his wings, he became afraid. The great expanse of sea stretched down beneath, and it was such a long way down - miles down. He felt certain that his wings would never support him, so he bent his head and ran away, back to the little hole under the ledge where he slept at night. Even when each of his brothers and his little sister, whose wings were far shorter than his own, ran to the brink, flapped their wings, and flew away, he failed to muster up the courage to take that plunge, which appeared to him so desperate. His father and mother had come around calling to him shrilly, upbraiding him, and threatening to let him starve on his ledge unless he flew away, but for the life of him, he could not move.

4. Part A
After reading the two passages, what contrast can be made?

Ⓐ Passage one is about an eagle, and passage two is about a seagull.
Ⓑ The eagle is old, and the seagull is young.
Ⓒ The old eagle has mastered flying whereas the young seagull is afraid of flying.
Ⓓ all of the above

4. Part B
While the eagle is a confident flyer, the seagull is _____.

Ⓐ Afraid to fly.
Ⓑ also a confident flyer.
Ⓒ A smaller bird.
Ⓓ Excited to fly.

4. Part C

The process of learning how to fly is discussed in _____.

   Ⓐ Both passages.
   Ⓑ Neither passage.
   Ⓒ "The Eagle"
   Ⓓ "First Flight"

RI.8.6 Author's Point of View

1. Which of the following is true of the point of view known as third-person omniscient?

(A) The narrator is not a character in the story.
(B) The narrator is a character in the story.
(C) The narrator only knows that he or she sees and hears.
(D) The narrator is talking about himself.

2. Which of the following is true of the point of view known as third-person limited?

(A) The narrator is not a character in the story.
(B) The narrator is a character in the story.
(C) The narrator only knows that he or she sees and hears.
(D) The narrator knows everything about all of the characters.

3 Which type of narrator is the most reliable?

(A) first person
(B) third person limited
(C) third person omniscient
(D) second person

You read a research study that says eating a candy bar made of dark chocolate every day is good for your heart in the long run. The study followed the health of a large group of people over the course of ten years. You notice in fine print at the end of the research that the study was conducted by a major chocolate company.

4. What might you, as a critical reader, take away from this?

Circle the correct answer choice.

(A) The study must be true if it is published.
(B) The conductors of the study benefit from the findings of this claim.
(C) Before believing this to be true, more studies need to be done by people who don't have stakes in a particular market.
(D) Both B and C

Name: _____   Date: _____

RI.8.7 Publishing Mediums

1. What is the best way to learn about WWII?

Ⓐ to watch movies
Ⓑ read nonfiction texts
Ⓒ read first-hand accounts published online
Ⓓ all of the above

2. You want to create a literary analysis of two novels. What is the best way to present this information?

Ⓐ in print
Ⓑ electronically
Ⓒ with pictures
Ⓓ online

3. Your teacher tells you that you must show a visual representation of a scene from a popular book. What is the best way to do this?

Ⓐ a movie
Ⓑ a play
Ⓒ an article
Ⓓ both A and B

4. What is the best place to search for a specific recipe you need in a hurry?

Circle the correct answer choice.

Ⓐ Internet
Ⓑ magazine
Ⓒ newspaper
Ⓓ recipe books

RI.8.8 Evaluating Authors Claims

1. Which of the following is the least acceptable piece of evidence?

- Ⓐ statistics
- Ⓑ quotes taken from a reliable source
- Ⓒ opinion
- Ⓓ facts

2. Emotional appeals (appealing to the reader's emotions) should...

- Ⓐ never be used
- Ⓑ be used sometimes
- Ⓒ should always be used
- Ⓓ are never appropriate

3. The author's evidence must...

- Ⓐ partially support the author's claims
- Ⓑ always be taken from a primary source
- Ⓒ directly support the author's claims
- Ⓓ all of the above

4. Determine whether the following statement is a fact, supported opinion, or unsupported opinion:

Texas is the hottest state in the United States.

Write your answer in the box given below.

_____

RI.8.9 Conflicting Information

1. Determine whether the conflicting information presented by the two authors is fact or interpretation.

Einstein
Albert Einstein was born on March 14th, 1879, in the German city of Ulm, without any indication that he was destined for greatness.
Einstein
Albert Einstein was born on March 15, 1879, in the city of Ulm. When he was born, people did not think he was going to be anything special.

  Ⓐ fact
  Ⓑ interpretation

2. Determine whether the following is fact or opinion.

Bailey is wearing blue shoes.

  Ⓐ fact
  Ⓑ opinion

3. Determine whether the following is fact or opinion.

Dr. Blair studied at the most prestigious schools, Harvard University.

  Write your answer in the box given below.

⎛⎯⎯⎯⎯⎯⎯⎯⎯⎯⎯⎯⎯⎯⎯⎯⎯⎯⎯⎯⎯⎞
⎝⎯⎯⎯⎯⎯⎯⎯⎯⎯⎯⎯⎯⎯⎯⎯⎯⎯⎯⎯⎯⎠

4. Determine whether the following is fact or opinion.

The atrocious painting sold for $1,000,000.

  Ⓐ fact
  Ⓑ opinion
  Ⓒ both

Answer Key and
Detailed Explanations

Reading: Informational Text

RI.8.1 Making Inferences Based on Textual Evidence

Question No.	Answer	Detailed Explanations
1.	A	Answer choice A is correct because it asked about the discovery, not actually trying to create. Answers B and C both have to do with experimenting, not discovering.
2.	B	Answer choice B is correct because it talks about the success of the experiment. Answer choice A is about the discovery of the idea, and answer choice C is about the trial and error of the experiment.
3.	C	Answer choice C is correct because it talks about how they tried "many more experiments".
4. Part A	D	Answer choice D is correct because it describes the first experiment the Montgolfier brothers did with a silk bag and fire. Answer choice A is incorrect because it provides information about the brothers' interests. Answer choice B is incorrect because it explains how Joseph Montgolfier conceived the idea of using hot air to propel an object. The idea came from an observation, not an experiment. Answer choice C is incorrect because it refers to other experiments, not the first one.
4. Part B	B	Answer choice B is correct because it shows how Joseph observed something as small as pieces of paper floating up the chimney. Answer choice A is incorrect because it describes the materials used to build the balloon. Answer choice C is incorrect because there is no text evidence to support this answer. The passage does not indicate that the Montgolfier's village was the best place to launch their balloon. Answer choice D is incorrect because it simply gives the reader information about Josepeh Montgolfier's interest in flying.

RI.8.2 Central Idea

Question No.	Answer	Detailed Explanations
1.	C	Answer choice C is correct. Emperor penguins lay their eggs in the Antarctic and take turns caring for the egg until it hatches. Answer choice A is incorrect because it is not the central idea of the text. Answer choice B is incorrect because the central idea includes both the location and caring of the egg.
2.	B	Answer choice B is correct. The central idea of this piece of informational text is the study of archaeology. Answer choice A is incorrect because the central idea is not the origin of archaeology as the origins are uncertain. Answer choice C is incorrect because the text is not at all about anthropology. Answer choice D is incorrect because the text is not only about the study of the human past.
3.	A	Answer choice A is correct. Archaeologists study past human life and culture by examining the things left behind by early humans. Answer choice B is incorrect because archaeologists study humans and their culture. Answer choice C is incorrect because archaeologists study not only humans and possibly their families, but also their culture.
4. Part A	D	Answer choice D is correct. When trying to determine the central idea of a passage, it is important to read the title, to read the passage, and pay close attention to the details which should support the central idea.
4. Part B	C	Answer choice C is correct. The passage is mainly about what it takes to prepare for and run a marathon. Most of the details support the central idea of preparing for and running a marathon.

RI.8.3 Connections and Distinctions

Question No.	Answer	Detailed Explanations
1.	A	Answer choice A is correct because the text points out one distinction between the types of quinoa.
2. Part A	D	Answer D is correct. They are many ways that marathons are different than other competitions.
2. Part B	A	Answer A is correct. The article mentions in the beginning that it's not competitive; therefore, answers B and C are incorrect.
3.	B	Answer B is correct. To find distinctions is to find differences.
4.	A	Answer choice A is correct. A connection is a similarity between the reader and something he understands.

RI.8.4 Determining Meaning of Words

Question No.	Answer	Detailed Explanations
1. Part A	C	Answer choice C is correct. To over exert means to do more than your body can handle.
1. Part B	A	Answer choice A is correct. In the spur of moment means taking immediate decisions without thinking. In this context also it means that training for marathon requires determination, hard work and commitment and it cannot be something that can be done instantaneously.
2.	C	Answer choice C is correct. To trek means to walk a long distance.
3.	B	Answer choice B is correct. A connotation is the meaning of the word with regard to its use in context.
4.	A	Detonation means the actual meaning of a word. In other words, it is the dictionary definition of the word. Hence, answer choice A is correct.

RI.8.5 Analyzing Structures in Text

Question No.	Answer	Detailed Explanations
1.	A	Answer choice A is correct. Adding an introductory and concluding paragraph would turn this passage into an essay. Remember an essay must have an introduction, body, and conclusion.
2.	A	Answer choice A is correct. The key words are first, soon afterwards, after this, and eventually. These words indicate a sequence of event.
3.	C	Answer choice C is correct. The passage was written to describe the egg laying routine of the Emperor Penguin. There are no clue words to lead the reader to believe there is any sequencing, comparing/ contrasting, or cause/effect included in the passage.
4. Part A	D	Answer choice D is correct. All three statements reflect differences, or contrasts, in the text.
4. Part B	A	Answer choice A is correct. The eagle is a confident flyer, but the seagull is afraid to leave the ledge. Answer choices B, C, and D are incorrect.
4. Part C	B	Answer choice B is correct. Neither passage discusses the process of flying.

RI.8.6 Author's Point of View

Question No.	Answer	Detailed Explanations
1.	A	Answer choice A is correct. A third person omniscient narrator is not included as a character in the story. The third person omniscient narrator knows the thoughts and feelings of all the characters in the story.
2.	A	Answer choice A is correct. A third person limited narrator is not a character in the story. The third person limited narrator only knows the thoughts and feelings of one character. This is unlike the third person omniscient narrator who knows the thoughts and feelings of all the characters.
3.	C	Answer choice C is correct. The most reliable narrator is the third person omniscient narrator because he or she knows the thoughts and feelings of all the characters.
4.	D	Answer choice D is correct. If the research was done by a company with ties to chocolate, chances are the data was collected or interpreted in a way to make it appear that eating chocolate is beneficial. It is best to rely on research conducted by independent research facilities.

RI.8.7 Publishing Mediums

Question No.	Answer	Detailed Explanations
1.	D	Answer choice D is correct. Remember, though, that movies will take liberties with facts. Primary sources will give accurate information, but you should incorporate nonfiction text in with your research, as well. Using as many data sources as possible in research will allow for a more thorough paper.
2.	A	Answer choice A is correct. The best way to present a literary analysis is in print, like an essay.
3.	D	Answer choice D is correct. The best way to show a visual representation of a book is via a short movie you film yourself or a play you create yourself.
4.	D	Answer choice A is correct. If you need a specific recipe in a hurry, the fastest place to get the information is by doing a web search on the Internet. You can use specific terms which should then navigate you to the appropriate sites.

RI.8.8 Evaluating Authors Claims

Question No.	Answer	Detailed Explanations
1.	C	Answer choice C is correct. An author who bases his or her claim primarily on opinion does not provide acceptable proof. Opinions are the least acceptable tools to use when making a claim.
2.	B	Answer choice B is correct. Emotional appeals should be used sparingly because, while they can be effective, they tend to be weak.
3.	C	Answer choice C is correct. Evidence used to support an author's claim should always be supportive of the claim.
4.	Unsupported opinion	While people who live in Texas may claim this to be true, this is an unsupported opinion.

RI.8.9 Conflicting Information

Question No.	Answer	Detailed Explanations
1.	A	Answer choice A is correct. Birthdates are verifiable; therefore, the conflicting information is based on fact. Additionally, the statements of what Einestein might be is documented fact.
2.	A	Answer choice A is correct. The color of Bailey's shoes can be proven.
3.	Both fact and opinion	There is both a fact and an opinion in the statement. Dr. Blair's university training can be verified, therefore, it is a fact. Whether or not Harvard is the most prestigious university is an opinion. Be careful you do not let a sentence with mixed information misguide you. Even in nonfiction, authors have bias.
4.	C	Answer choice C is correct. Evidently the person who purchased the painting for $1,000,000 (which is verifiable) did not believe the painting to be atrocious. Therefore, the statement included both a fact and an opinion.

Language

The objective of the Language standards is to ensure that the student is able to accurately use grade appropriate general academic and domain specific words and phrases.
To help students to master the necessary skills, we encourage the student to go through the resources available online on Lumos EdSearch to gain an in depth understanding of these concepts.

L.8.1.A   Adjectives and Adverbs

1. Which choice is the adverb that correctly completes the following sentence?

I am very fond of Miss Jenkins; she teaches very _____.

- Ⓐ patiently
- Ⓑ patient
- Ⓒ patience
- Ⓓ patiented

2. Which word is the adverb in the following sentence?

She picked up the sweet baby very carefully.

- Ⓐ sweet
- Ⓑ very
- Ⓒ carefully
- Ⓓ both B and C

3. Which word in the following sentence is an adjective?

After a long afternoon at practice, I am tired, hungry, and dirty.

- Ⓐ tired
- Ⓑ hungry
- Ⓒ dirty
- Ⓓ all of the above

4. What is the adjective in the following sentence?

Greg bounced around the playground, happily playing on his new slide.

Write your answer in the box given below.

LumosLearning.com

L.8.1.B Subject-Verb Agreement

1. Select the correct verb form to agree with the subject in the following sentence.

The highlighter or the marker _____ in the side drawer.

    Ⓐ is
    Ⓑ are
    Ⓒ rolling
    Ⓓ writing

2. Select the correct verb form to agree with the subject in the following sentence.

The student, along with his parents, _____ coming to the talent show.

    Ⓐ is
    Ⓑ are
    Ⓒ never
    Ⓓ walking

3. Select the correct verb form to agree with the subject in the following sentence.

Neither the tomatoes nor the mint in my garden _____ begun to grow.

    Ⓐ has
    Ⓑ have
    Ⓒ it doesn't matter which verb form is used

4. Fill in the blank with the correct verb.

The boys and girls _____ very excited about the trip next week.

L.8.1.C Pronouns

1 Choose the correct pronoun in the sentence below.

With (who/whom) were you speaking?

Ⓐ who
Ⓑ whom

2. Choose the correct pronoun in the sentence below.

(Who/whom) can you send to help us?

Ⓐ who
Ⓑ whom

3. Identify the pronoun in the following sentence.

Martha's sister wanted her siblings to give her something exciting for her birthday.

Ⓐ Martha
Ⓑ sister
Ⓒ birthday
Ⓓ her

4. Fill in the blank with the correct pronoun:

Julie couldn't believe _____ friend didn't listen to _____ advice.

L.8.1.C Phrases and Clauses

1. What is a subordinate clause?

Ⓐ It has a subject and verb and can be a complete sentence by itself.
Ⓑ It has a subject and a verb but cannot stand by itself as a complete sentence.
Ⓒ It is only two words.
Ⓓ It does not have either a subject or a verb and is, therefore, not a sentence.

2. What is an adjective phrase?

Ⓐ It modifies a noun.
Ⓑ It modifies a verb, adverb, or adjective.
Ⓒ It tells "what kind" or "which one."
Ⓓ both A and C

3. What does the following sentence contain?

The dog with the bright blue collar jumped on me.

Ⓐ an adverb phrase
Ⓑ an adjective phrase

4. Is the clause in the following sentence independent or subordinate?

My son, an accomplished fisherman, caught the largest fish in the tournament.

L.8.1.D Verbals

1. Which of the following sentences uses the verbal known as a participle?

Ⓐ After school, my friends and I are going to go to the mall.
Ⓑ The soup boiling on the stove smells delicious.
Ⓒ I walked my dog around the block.
Ⓓ My friends are coming over after school today.

2. What part of speech is the verbal taking in the following sentence?

The sparkling ring is beautiful.

Ⓐ noun
Ⓑ adjective
Ⓒ verb
Ⓓ adverb

3. What part of speech is the verbal taking in the following sentence?

The bird was sleeping in its nest.

Ⓐ noun
Ⓑ adjective
Ⓒ verb
Ⓓ adverb

4. What part of speech is the verbal taking in the following sentence?

Jogging is my least favorite cardio activity.

Circle the correct answer choice.

Ⓐ noun
Ⓑ adjective
Ⓒ adverbial

L.8.3.A Active and Passive Voice

1. Is the following sentence written in active or passive voice?

Samantha sewed the hem of her sister's wedding dress when it ripped.

Ⓐ active
Ⓑ passive
Ⓒ neither
Ⓓ both

2. Which of the following sentences is written in active voice?

a) One day that dress will be handed down to me by my mother.
b) My father always changes the oil in our vehicles by himself.
c) I made chocolate chip cookies for the birthday party.
d) That cabinet was made by my grandfather.

Ⓐ a and b
Ⓑ b and c
Ⓒ d and c
Ⓓ a and d

3. Which of the following sentences are written in an active voice?

a) This house was built by my uncle.
b) This wonderful dessert was baked by my mother.

Ⓐ a
Ⓑ b
Ⓒ both a and b
Ⓓ none of the above

4. Identify whether the following sentence is written in the active or passive voice.

Much to her mother's dismay, Chloe colored on the dining room table.

Write your answer in the box given below.

L.8.2.A Punctuation

1. Determine which sentence shows the correct usage of the apostrophe and comma.

- Ⓐ I couldn't wait to see Katie's new dog, Alfie.
- Ⓑ I couldn't wait to see Katies new dog, Alfie.
- Ⓒ I couldn't wait to see Katie new dog Alfie.
- Ⓓ I couldn't wait to see Katie's new dog Alfie.

2. Which of the following does the contraction "would've" take the place of?

- Ⓐ would of
- Ⓑ would have
- Ⓒ will of
- Ⓓ will have

3. Punctuate the below sentence.

Yvettes invitation for Brendas surprise party said to bring the following things to the party cupcakes soda and a gag gift.

4. Where would you include a dash in the following sentence?

Kasey had not taken the time to read the directions no wonder the bookcase fell apart after an hour!

L.8.2.B Ellipsis

1. If an ellipsis comes at the end of the sentence, add it after the period for a total of 4 dots, so it looks like this....
Mark "True" or "False"

Ⓐ True
Ⓑ False

2. The following is the correct use of an ellipsis.
I don't know...I'm not sure...What do you think?
Mark "True" or "False"

Ⓐ True
Ⓑ False

3. When is it appropriate to use an ellipsis?

Ⓐ when citing evidence from a text that is long
Ⓑ when researching and information is at the beginning and end of a paragraph
Ⓒ when trying to be concise and only use necessary facts
Ⓓ all of the above

4. What is the appropriate way to cite the following information?

It was a dark and stormy night. The people of Cape Hatteras hid indoors. Mrs. Peabody shivered, hoping the hurricane would not visit and wondering whether she would be able to fall asleep. Across the street, Mr. Greer kept watch from the high tower of his attic, certain that the hurricane would strike soon.

Ⓐ The newspaper reported on the hurricane. The writer explained, "The people of Cape Hatteras hid indoors. ... Mr. Greer kept watch from the high tower of his attic...."
Ⓑ The newspaper reported on the hurricane. The writer explained, "The people of Cape Hatteras hid indoors; Mr. Greer kept watch from the high tower of his attic...."
Ⓒ The newspaper reported on the hurricane. The writer explained, "The people of Cape Hatteras hid indoors. Mr. Greer kept watching from the high tower of his attic...."
Ⓓ none of the above

L.8.2.C Spelling

1. Which word(s) in the following paragraph are misspelled?

I was trying to acommodate all of my friends. They were all coming to my birthday party, and I wanted to insure that I had the coolest prizes for the winners of the games; I made sure their were enough prizes for everyone.

    Ⓐ acommodate
    Ⓑ insure
    Ⓒ their
    Ⓓ all of the above

2. What is the correct spelling for the misspelled word in the sentence below?

Usually, I like to read on the beach; however, occationally I will swim.

    Ⓐ usualy
    Ⓑ beech
    Ⓒ occasionally
    Ⓓ how ever

3. What is the correct spelling for the misspelled word in the sentence below?

It is unclear whether or not I will go on vacation with my family.

    Ⓐ weather
    Ⓑ knot
    Ⓒ vacetion
    Ⓓ none of the above

4. What is the correct spelling for the misspelled word in the sentence below?

I am going to perswade my mother to buy me a dog.

L.8.3.A Mood in Verbs

1. The subjunctive mood of a verb does what?

- Ⓐ gives a command
- Ⓑ states a fact
- Ⓒ expresses a wish
- Ⓓ states a condition

2. Part A
Which of the following sentences is written in the subjunctive mood?

- Ⓐ It will rain tomorrow.
- Ⓑ It might rain tomorrow.
- Ⓒ Prepare for the rain tomorrow.
- Ⓓ none of the above

2. Part B
Which of the following sentences is written in the imperative mood?

- Ⓐ It will rain tomorrow.
- Ⓑ It might rain tomorrow.
- Ⓒ Prepare for the rain tomorrow.
- Ⓓ none of the above

3. Which of the following sentences is written in the indicative mood?

Circle the correct answer choice.

- Ⓐ It will rain tomorrow.
- Ⓑ It might rain tomorrow.
- Ⓒ Prepare for the rain tomorrow.
- Ⓓ none of the above

4. All verbs in the English language have which of the following?

- Ⓐ mood
- Ⓑ tense
- Ⓒ voice
- Ⓓ all of the above

L.8.4.A Context Clues

1. **Michael's overt flirting with Michelle during lunch drew the attention of Larry, her boyfriend.**

What is the best meaning of overt?

- Ⓐ concealed
- Ⓑ hidden
- Ⓒ obvious
- Ⓓ secret

2. **Vanity got the best of Sarah as she ran into the wall while checking her hair in the mirror at the end of the hallway.**

What is the best meaning of vanity?

- Ⓐ modestly
- Ⓑ pride in one's qualities
- Ⓒ lack of real value
- Ⓓ tried things in vain

3. **Becca's rude and pithy response to her teacher only took a second, but it landed her a week in after school detention.**

What is the best meaning of pithy?

- Ⓐ brief
- Ⓑ long winded
- Ⓒ sweet
- Ⓓ impolite

4. **What is the best definition of foreboding?**

Circle the correct answer choice.

- Ⓐ good fortune
- Ⓑ bad feeling
- Ⓒ fortune
- Ⓓ anticipation

L.8.4.B Multiple Meaning Words

1. Choose the word that is a synonym for the underlined word in the following sentence.

Amanda has not been feeling well lately. She went to visit her doctor today to <u>determine</u> why she has been under the weather.

- Ⓐ settle
- Ⓑ decline
- Ⓒ abstain
- Ⓓ study

2. What is the correct definition of the word "suit" as it is used in the sentence below?

When I decided not to go to the prom, my girlfriend said, "Suit yourself. I'll find someone else to dance with."

- Ⓐ formal attire
- Ⓑ legal action
- Ⓒ benefit
- Ⓓ request

3. What is the correct definition of the word "band" as it is used in the sentence below?

Let's band together to stamp out hunger!

- Ⓐ encircle
- Ⓑ a group of people with the same interest
- Ⓒ to come together
- Ⓓ a musical group

4. Which of the homophones, "complement" and "compliment," will correctly fit into the following sentence?

I like to wear my blue, flowered dress. Whenever I wear it, I receive a lot of _____ (s).

- Ⓐ compliment
- Ⓑ complement

L.8.4.B Roots, Affixes, and Syllables

1. Identify the affixes in the following words?

mislead, unrestricted, reiterate

- Ⓐ mis, un, re
- Ⓑ lead, ed, ate
- Ⓒ lead, stricted, rate
- Ⓓ lead, restricted, iterate

2. The root word, cede means, "to go." With this knowledge, determine the meaning of the word "precede."

- Ⓐ to go after
- Ⓑ to go away
- Ⓒ to go before
- Ⓓ to go never

3. Dynamic means physical force or energy. What does the root word "Dyna" mean?

- Ⓐ to be weak
- Ⓑ power
- Ⓒ to be little
- Ⓓ to be tired

4. Match the word to its meaning based on the suffix

	full of care	someone who applies for something	a person who specializes in studying the history of the earth, including rocks
The suffix "ist" means a skilled person in. a geologist is			
The suffix "ful" means full of. Therefore the word "careful" means:			
The suffix "ant" means a person who. Applicant means			

L.8.4.C Reference Materials

1 How can you determine whether a source is reliable?

Ⓐ If you obtained your information from the Internet, it is always reliable.
Ⓑ You should consider who wrote the source and why.
Ⓒ If you obtained your information from an actual article, it will be reliable.
Ⓓ answer choices B & C

2. Why must you be very careful about obtaining information from websites?

Ⓐ It can be difficult to find reputable sources.
Ⓑ Some sites can be edited by anyone.
Ⓒ It is too easy to find what may look like good information but sources are often unverifiable.
Ⓓ all of the above

3. What are the benefits of using primary sources?

Ⓐ They are first-hand accounts from those who witnessed or experienced the event being researched.
Ⓑ They offer a limited perspective.
Ⓒ They haven't been very well researched.
Ⓓ They have reposted hundreds of times.

4. Part A
What are primary sources?

Ⓐ materials that come directly from the source
Ⓑ materials that have been copied from the source
Ⓒ materials that are found only in encyclopedias
Ⓓ materials that are over 100 years old

4. Part B
Which of the following are examples of secondary sources?

Ⓐ biographies
Ⓑ encyclopedias
Ⓒ textbooks
Ⓓ documentaries
Ⓔ all of the above

L.8.4.D Using Context to Verify Meaning

Marathon

Training for a marathon takes hard work and **perseverance**. It is not something you can do on the **spur** of the moment. Preparing for a marathon takes months, particularly if you have never run a marathon before. The official distance of a full marathon is 26.2 miles. In 2005, the average time to complete a marathon in the United States was 4 hours 32 minutes 8 seconds for men and 5 hours 6 minutes 8 seconds for women.

Most people who run marathons are not trying to win. Many runners try to beat their own best time. Some compare their time to other runners in the same gender and age group. Some people set time-oriented goals, such as finishing under four hours, while others try to complete the race without slowing to a walk. Many beginners simply hope to finish the marathon.

Trainers recommend that beginners maintain a **consistent** running schedule for six weeks prior to even starting a marathon training program. The purpose of this is to allow the body to adapt to the **various** physical demands of long-distance running. First-time marathon runners should train by running four days a week for at least four months, increasing distance by no more than ten percent weekly. As race day approaches, runners should **taper** their runs, reducing the strain on their bodies and resting before the marathon. It is important not to over**exert** yourself during training because that can lead to a lot of injuries. Most common injuries are spraining of the knees and ankles. These sprains can **hinder** the training.

Before the race, it is important to stretch in order to keep muscles **limber**. Staying hydrated is also important, but there is a danger in drinking too much water. If a runner drinks too much water, they may experience a dangerous condition called **hyponatremia**, a drop of sodium levels in the blood. During the race, trainers recommend maintaining a steady pace. It is normal to feel sore after a marathon. Light exercise will help sore muscles heal faster.

Some people run marathons in pairs or groups. Training for and running a marathon with another person or group of people can make the experience more enjoyable and more rewarding. A running partner might be just the motivation you need to show up for an early morning run instead of rolling over to hit the snooze button. And, when you cross the finish line together, you can share the satisfaction of reaching your common goal.

Usually, thousands of people sign up and run a marathon. Most people finish the race. The thrill of running a marathon for the first time is unbelievable. The training sessions are harder if you have never run before. But it is unbelievable what ones' body can do when one puts his/her mind to it. Having a good coach to support you makes all the difference in training for a marathon.

The daily runs are very important. Strength training and core training are also very important.

Using context clues in the story, determine the meaning of the bold words.

1. various

    Ⓐ many
    Ⓑ few
    Ⓒ hard
    Ⓓ simple

2. taper

    Ⓐ add more
    Ⓑ pick and choose
    Ⓒ scale back
    Ⓓ candle

3. exert

    Ⓐ sleep
    Ⓑ utilize
    Ⓒ rest
    Ⓓ run

4. "If you cannot determine a word's meaning in context, where can you look?
From among the 4 choices given below, select the correct answer and enter it in the box given below."

    Ⓐ thesaurus
    Ⓑ dictionary
    Ⓒ encyclopedia
    Ⓓ journal

L.8.5.A Interpreting Figures of Speech

1. Today, my brother and I went to the batting cages. I was in awe of him as I watched him hit ball after ball; he was a machine.

   Why is the brother being compared to a machine?

   Ⓐ He seemed to be under the control of a robot.
   Ⓑ He hit every ball with accuracy and efficiency.
   Ⓒ He was rigid and metal-like.
   Ⓓ He didn't show much emotion as he hit the balls.

2. **What is the meaning of the following metaphor?**

   He has the heart of a lion.

   Ⓐ the people on the street
   Ⓑ He is hairy.
   Ⓒ He has a large heart.
   Ⓓ He is courageous.

3. **What figure of speech is used in the following sentence?**

   The leaves of the tree danced in the breeze.

   Ⓐ personification
   Ⓑ metaphor
   Ⓒ simile
   Ⓓ idiom

4. **What figure of speech is used in the following sentence:**

   Sarah was like a toddler hungry for food; I was ready to get out of the car with her.

   Write your answer in the box given below.

L.8.5.B Relationships Between Words

1. Study the analogy below to determine the relationship between the words that are presented.

won is to one as the rode is to road

- Ⓐ homonyms
- Ⓑ synonyms
- Ⓒ homophones
- Ⓓ homographs

2. Study the analogy below to determine the relationship between the words that are presented.

A woman is to women as mouse is to mice

- Ⓐ present tense to past tense
- Ⓑ singular to plural
- Ⓒ plural to singular
- Ⓓ antonyms

3. Finish the following analogy.

tiny is too small as enormous is to

- Ⓐ minute
- Ⓑ monstrous
- Ⓒ large
- Ⓓ petite

4. Match and write the word to it's definition

Analogy ——

Antonyms ——

Synonyms ——

Definitions:

1. Words that mean the same thing
2. Words with opposite meanings
3. A comparison of two words

L.8.5.C Denotations and Connotations

1. What is a negative connotation for funny?

Ⓐ absurd
Ⓑ uncommon
Ⓒ comical
Ⓓ amusing

2. What would a negative connotation for the word "quick" be?

Ⓐ prompt
Ⓑ rapid
Ⓒ hasty
Ⓓ responsive

3. What is a neutral connotation for small?

Ⓐ short
Ⓑ paltry
Ⓒ insignificant
Ⓓ trivial

4. Part A
What is the definition of <u>denotation</u>?

Ⓐ the feelings or ideas a word suggests
Ⓑ the actual dictionary definition of a word
Ⓒ a word that is a symbol of the opposite word
Ⓓ words that have the same meanings

4. Part B
What is the definition of <u>connotation</u>?

Ⓐ the feelings or ideas a word suggests
Ⓑ the actual dictionary definition of a word
Ⓒ a word that is a symbol of the opposite word
Ⓓ a word that means the same thing

L.8.6 Domain Specific Words

1. What word in the following sentence is a domain-specific vocabulary word?

The slope of the line is calculated using the slope-intercept form. It is important to understand this formula if you want to be a successful math student.

- Ⓐ student
- Ⓑ successful
- Ⓒ calculated
- Ⓓ important

2. What word in the following sentence is a domain-specific vocabulary word?

The economy is governed by supply and demand. The market is what drives the economy, and the economy is what capitalism is based upon.

- Ⓐ market
- Ⓑ economy
- Ⓒ capitalism
- Ⓓ all of the above

3. What word in the following sentence is a domain-specific vocabulary word?

The poem can be interpreted in many ways. Readers can begin their interpretation by looking at a poem's meter, and then by closely examining its rhyme scheme and its rhythm. The overall interpretation should include the many nuances of the poem.

- Ⓐ interpreted
- Ⓑ meter
- Ⓒ nuances
- Ⓓ closely

4. What word in the following sentence is a domain-specific vocabulary word?

Look closely to see that the plugs and plug wires are all in good shape. Do this simple check before taking your car to the mechanic, and it might save you a few bucks. Keep your money in your pocket if you can.

L.8.2 Capitalization

1. Which of the following words should always be capitalized?

Ⓐ Grandmother
Ⓑ the first word of every sentence
Ⓒ names of subjects, such as Science
Ⓓ all of the above

2. What is the correct way to capitalize "grandmother" in the below sentences?

a. We should go to visit (grandmother/ Grandmother) today.
b. This weekend we went to see my (grandmother/ Grandmother).

Ⓐ grandmother, grandmother
Ⓑ Grandmother, grandmother
Ⓒ grandmother, Grandmother
Ⓓ None of the above

3. Which words need to be capitalized in the following sentences?

next week, my report on wwll is due. I have an awful lot of studying and research to complete; it looks like I will spending a lot of time at the Joann Darcy public library.

Ⓐ next
Ⓑ wwll
Ⓒ public library
Ⓓ all of the above

4. Which word should be capitalized in the following sentence?

Betty and I are going to france for spring break.

Write your answer in the box given below.

```
┌─────────────────────────────────────┐
│                                      │
│                                      │
└─────────────────────────────────────┘
```

Answer Key and
Detailed Explanations

Language

L.8.1.A Adjectives and Adverbs

Question No.	Answer	Detailed Explanations
1.	A	Answer choice A is correct. The word "patiently" is an adverb describing how Miss Jenkins teaches.
2.	D	Answer choice D is correct. The words "very" and "carefully" are both adverbs which describe how the baby was picked up.
3.	D	Answer choice D is correct. The adjectives "tired, dirty, and hungry" describe how the narrator feels after a long afternoon at practice.
4.	new	The word "new" describes the slide.

L.8.1.B Subject-Verb Agreement

Question No.	Answer	Detailed Explanations
1.	A	Answer choice A is correct. When two or more singular nouns are connected with "or" or "nor" use a singular verb.
2.	A	Answer choice A is correct. The subject of this sentence is "the student," which is singular, so the verb must also be singular. Be careful with sentences that put a phrase in between the subject and the verb.
3.	A	Answer choice A is correct. When there is more than one subject, one being singular and one being plural, the verb matches the subject closest to it.
4.	are	The nouns in the subject are plural; therefore the verb must also be plural.

L.8.1.C Pronouns

Question No.	Answer	Detailed Explanations
1.	B	Answer choice B is correct. "Who" is a subject pronoun and "whom" is an object pronoun. In the sentence above, the word "you" is the subject, and "whom" is the direct object. A test to determine which pronoun to use is to substitute the words "who" and "whom" with "she" and "her". Whenever the word "she" is appropriate, the pronoun "who" can be used. Whenever the word "her" is appropriate, the word "whom" can be used. You would apply this test to the sentence by asking the question, "Who am I speaking with?" To which the answer would be, "I am speaking with her". According to the test, we would use the pronoun, "whom".
2.	B	Answer choice B is correct. Who is a subject pronoun and whom is an object pronoun. The subject of the sentence above is you, so we know that the answer is whom because it is the direct object. A test to determine which pronoun to use is to substitute the words who and whom with she and her. Whenever the word she is appropriate, the pronoun who can be used. Whenever the word her can be used, the pronoun whom can be used. You would apply this to the sentence above by answering the question which is being asked. The answer would be, "They are sending her to help us". According to the test we would use the pronoun, whom.
3.	D	Answer choice D is correct. The pronoun "her" is used three times and refers to Martha.
4.	her, her	The pronoun "her" is used twice and refers to Julie.

L.8.1.C Phrases and Clauses

Question No.	Answer	Detailed Explanations
1.	B	Answer choice B is correct. A subordinate clause, also known as a dependent clause, has a subject and a verb but cannot stand by itself as a complete sentence.
2.	C	Answer choice C is correct. An adjective phrase modifies a noun and tells "what kind" or "which one."
3.	B	Answer choice B is correct. The adjective phrase is "with the bright blue collar." It describes (tells which one) the dog.
4.	subordinate	The clause is "an accomplished fisherman." It cannot stand alone; therefore, it is subordinate (or dependent).

L.8.1.D Verbals

Question No.	Answer	Detailed Explanations
1.	B	Answer choice B is correct. The participle, "boiling on the stove," describes the soup.
2.	B	Answer choice B is correct. The word "sparkling" describes the ring; therefore, it works as an adjective in this sentence.
3.	C	Answer choice C is correct. The word "sleeping" functions as a verb in the sentence.
4.	A	Answer choice A is correct. The word "jogging" functions as a noun in this sentence.

L.8.3.A Active and Passive Voice

Question No.	Answer	Detailed Explanations
1.	A	Answer choice A is correct. The correct answer is active. The subject of the sentence is Samantha, as she is doing the action, and she is treated as the subject. If this sentence were passive it would read, "The wedding dress was sewn by Samantha." The answer could not be neither, because a sentence is ALWAYS either active or passive.
2.	B	Answer choice B is correct. Both B and C are written in active voice. The sentences show that the subjects are doing the action.
3.	D	Answer choice D is correct. Both of the above sentences are written in passive voice. In both examples, the objects are being treated as the subject.
4.	Active	The subject is doing the action.

L.8.2.A Punctuation

Question No.	Answer	Detailed Explanations
1.	A	Answer choice A is correct. Commas should be used to separate a series of words or word groups, between two independent clauses joined by a coordinating conjunction (and, or, but, for, nor), and in a date between the day and year. These are not all the comma rules, but they are the rules that are mostly commonly broken.
2.	B	Answer choice B is correct. The missing, or omitted, letters are "h" and "a". The word "would've" is a contraction for the words "would have".
3.	--	Correct Answer- Yvette's invitation for Brenda's surprise party said to bring the following things to the party: cupcakes, soda, and a gag gift. Both names are possessive; a colon is used because a list follows, and commas separate the list.
4.	--	Correct Answer- Kasey had not taken the time to read the directions - no wonder the bookcase fell apart after an hour! The dash takes the place of a semicolon in this example. Remember to use dashes sparingly and not in formal writing.

L.8.2.B Ellipsis

Question No.	Answer	Detailed Explanations
1.	A	Answer choice A is correct. The statement above is true.
2.	A	Answer choice A is correct. An ellipsis in dialogue can indicate a pause.
3.	D	Answer choice D is correct. In all of the above examples, an ellipsis would be used.
4.	A	Answer choice A is correct. The ellipsis indicates that areas of the text have been omitted.

L.8.2.C Spelling

Question No.	Answer	Detailed Explanations
1.	D	Answer choice D is correct. Answer choice A is spelled accommodate. Answer choice B is a homophone; the correct word is ensure. Answer choice C is also a homophone and should be spelled there.
2.	C	Answer choice C is correct. The correct spelling is occasionally.
3.	D	Answer choice D is correct. No words are misused or misspelled.
4.	persuade	The correct spelling is persuade.

L.8.3.A Mood in Verbs

Question No.	Answer	Detailed Explanations
1.	C	Answer choice C is correct. The subjunctive form of a verb expresses anything uncertain. Since a wish is uncertain, it is in a subjunctive mood.
2. Part A	B	Answer choice B is correct because it expresses an uncertainty.
2. Part B	C	Answer choice C is correct. An imperative tone gives a command, and answer choice C is giving a command.
3.	A	Answer choice A is correct because an indicative tone indicates a fact.
4.	D	Answer choice D is correct. Verbs have mood, tense, and voice.

L.8.4.A Context Clues

Question No.	Answer	Detailed Explanations
1.	C	Answer choice C is correct. Michael's overt flirting with Michelle during lunch drew the attention of Larry, her boyfriend.
2.	B	Answer choice B is correct. Vanity got the best of Sarah as she ran into the wall while checking her hair in the mirror at the end of the hallway.
3.	A	Answer choice A is correct. Becca's rude and pithy response to her teacher only took a second, but it landed her a week in after school detention.
4.	B	Answer choice B is correct. Context clues are underlined in the sentences: Bailey had a sense of foreboding as she walked into the classroom. She noticed that all the bulletin boards were covered up and the privacy folders were lying on the desks. Had she forgotten a test?

L.8.4.B Multiple Meaning Words

Question No.	Answer	Detailed Explanations
1.	A	Answer choice A is correct. Determine has many meanings, but within the context of the sentence, only A is correct.
2.	C	Answer choice C is correct. Suit, in this case, means benefit, as in benefit or be happy with your own decision.
3.	C	Answer choice C is correct. While all the definitions for band are correct, within the context of this sentence, only answer choice C is correct.
4.	A	Answer choice A is correct. The definition of compliment is: praise. The definition of complement is: add to in a way that enhances or improves a thing.

L.8.4.B Roots, Affixes, and Syllables

Question No.	Answer	Detailed Explanations
1.	A	Answer choice A is correct. Mis, un, and re are prefixes. Prefixes are also known as affixes. Suffixes are also affixes.
2.	C	Answer choice C is correct. The prefix "pre" means before. If cede means to, then when combined, the word prefix means to go before.
3.	B	Answer choice B is correct. The root word "dyna" means power. Other words that include the root word dyna are: dynamite and dynamo.
4.	--	Geologist - a person who specializes in studying the history of the earth, including rocks careful - full of care applicant - someone who applies for something

L.8.4.C Reference Materials

Question No.	Answer	Detailed Explanations
1.	B	Answer choice B is correct. It is difficult to determine the reliability of one or two sources. When doing research, it is important to constantly ask yourself who wrote the resources you are using and why were they written? Using several sources for research will prove to be most reliable.
2.	D	Answer choice D is correct. Use caution when using Internet resources. Make sure the author is reliable and the information is current.
3.	A	Answer choice A. The benefit of using a primary source is that the account from the source actually witnessed or experienced the event being researched.
4. Part A	A	Answer choice A is correct. Primary sources are those that come directly from the source.
4. Part B	E	Answer choice E is correct. Secondary sources interpret and analyze primary sources.

L.8.4.D Using Context to Verify Meaning

Question No.	Answer	Detailed Explanations
1.	A	Answer choice A is correct. Because the context says "demands" not "demand" readers know there are many.
2.	C	Answer choice C is correct. Some of the words in context like "reducing" and "relaxing" show readers that "taper" means to scale back.
3.	B	Answer choice B is correct. The context of "leading to injuries" helps reader understand not to push too hard; hence, utilize.
4.	B	Answer choice B is correct. A dictionary is the right choice.

L.8.5.A Interpreting Figures of Speech

Question No.	Answer	Detailed Explanations
1.	B	Answer choice B is correct. This sentence uses a simile to compare the speaker's brother to a machine. Because of the simile, the reader can determine the brother hit the ball flawlessly, like a machine designed to hit balls would. Answer choices A, C, and D are incorrect.
2.	D	Answer choice D is correct. Lions are thought to be courageous, so someone with a lion's heart is courageous. Answer choices A, B, and C are incorrect.
3.	A	Answer choice A is correct. The ability to dance is a human characteristic; therefore, the leaves dancing are an example of personification. Answer choices B, C, and D are incorrect.
4.	simile	Sarah is being compared to a hungry toddler. When toddlers are hungry, they are cranky and generally cry and carry on.

L.8.5.B Relationships Between Words

Question No.	Answer	Detailed Explanations
1.	C	Answer choice C is correct. The word pairs are homophones meaning each pair sounds the same but are spelled differently and have different meanings. Answer choices A, B, and D are incorrect.
2.	B	Answer choice B is correct. The analogy includes pairs of words are singular and plural. Answer choices A, C, and D are incorrect.
3.	C	Answer choice C is correct. "Tiny" and "small" are synonyms so the word pair must also be synonyms. While "enormous" and "monstrous" could be considered synonyms, the word "large" is a better choice. You must look more at the analogy and notice that the first words in the pair are antonyms: "tiny" and "enormous". Keeping that in mind, the best antonym pair for the second set of words is "small" and "large". Answer choices A and D are incorrect.
4.	--	Analogy - a comparison of two words Antonyms - words with opposite meanings Synonyms - words that mean the same thing

L.8.5.C Denotations and Connotations

Question No.	Answer	Detailed Explanations
1.	A	Answer choice A is correct. The word "absurd" is a synonym for funny, but means something unreasonably funny. Answer choices B, C, and D are incorrect because they are all words with positive connotations.
2.	C	Answer choice C is correct. The word "hasty" is used when a decision is made quickly without much thought. Answer choices A, B, and D are incorrect because they are words with positive connotations.
3.	A	Answer choice A is correct. The word "short" has a neutral connotation and generally stays neutral within surrounding text. Answer choices B, C, and D all carry negative connotations.
4. Part A	B	Answer choice B is correct. One way to remember that denotation refers to the dictionary definition of a word is to remember that they both begin with the letter "d". Answer choices A is incorrect. Connotation means the feelings or ideas a word suggests. Answer choices C and D are incorrect.
4. Part B	A	Answer choice A is correct. The connotation (suggested meaning) of a word can change, depending on how it is used in a sentence. Connotations are usually described as positive or negative. Answer choice B is the definition of denotation. Answer choices C and D are incorrect.

L.8.6 Domain Specific Words

Question No.	Answer	Detailed Explanations
1.	C	Answer choice C is correct. A calculation is specific to math; therefore, it is domain specific.
2.	D	Answer choice D is correct. All of the choices relate to economics; therefore, they are all domain specific.
3.	B	Answer choice B is correct. Meter is specific to poetry; therefore, it is domain specific.
4.	--	Plugs are specific to cars; therefore, it is domain specific.

L.8.2 Capitalization

Question No.	Answer	Detailed Explanations
1.	B	Answer choice B is correct. The first word of every sentence should ALWAYS be capitalized. Answer choice A, grandmother, would be capitalized when it is used as a proper noun. Proper nouns should always be capitalized.
2.	B	Answer choice B is correct. In the first sentence, the word "grandmother" is used as a proper noun.
3.	D	Answer choice D is correct. Always capitalize historical events, the first letter of a sentence, and all words in the title or name of an organization.
4.	France	Only the proper noun, France, should be capitalized. Remember seasons are not capitalized.

Additional Information

What if I buy more than one Lumos Study Program?

Step 1

Visit the URL and login to your account.
http://www.lumoslearning.com

Step 2

Click on 'My tedBooks' under the "Account" tab.
Place the Book Access Code and submit.

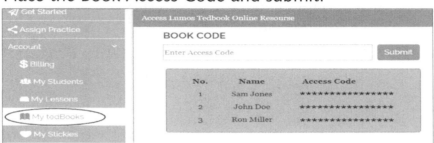

Step 3

To add the new book for a registered student, choose the
○ Existing Student button and select the student and submit.

To add the new book for a new student, choose the ○ Add New student
button and complete the student registration.

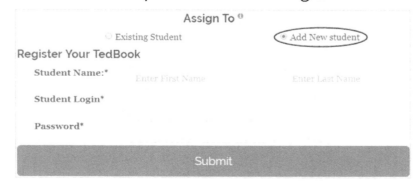

Lumos StepUp® Mobile App
FAQ For Students

What is the Lumos StepUp® App?

It is a FREE application you can download onto your Android Smartphones, tablets, iPhones, and iPads.

What are the Benefits of the StepUp® App?

This mobile application gives convenient access to Practice Tests, Common Core State Standards, Online Workbooks, and learning resources through your Smartphone and tablet computers.

- Eleven Technology enhanced question types in both MATH and ELA
- Sample questions for Arithmetic drills
- Standard specific sample questions
- Instant access to the Common Core State Standards
- Jokes and cartoons to make learning fun!

Do I Need the StepUp® App to Access Online Workbooks?

No, you can access Lumos StepUp® Online Workbooks through a personal computer. The StepUp® app simply enhances your learning experience and allows you to conveniently access StepUp® Online Workbooks and additional resources through your smartphone or tablet.

How can I Download the App?

Visit **lumoslearning.com/a/stepup-app** using your Smartphone or tablet and follow the instructions to download the app.

QR Code
for Smartphone
Or Tablet Users

Lumos StepUp® Mobile App FAQ For Parents and Teachers

What is the Lumos StepUp® App?

It is a free app that teachers can use to easily access real-time student activity information as well as assign learning resources to students. Parents can also use it to easily access school-related information such as homework assigned by teachers and PTA meetings. It can be downloaded onto smartphones and tablets from popular App Stores.

What are the Benefits of the Lumos StepUp® App?

It provides convenient access to

- Standards aligned learning resources for your students
- An easy to use Dashboard
- Student progress reports
- Active and inactive students in your classroom
- Professional development information
- Educational Blogs

How can I Download the App?

Visit **lumoslearning.com/a/stepup-app** using your Smartphone or tablet and follow the instructions to download the app.

**QR Code
for Smartphone
Or Tablet Users**

GRADE 8 >>> 9

Lumos Learning
Developed by Expert Teachers

BACK TO SCHOOL
REFRESHER
MATH

★ **Grade 8 Review**   ★ **Preview of Grade 9**

Measure and Remediate Learning Loss

Diagnose Learning Gaps

Get Targeted Practice

Prepare for Grade 9

Updated for 2021-22

(((tedBook)))

Includes Additional Online Practice

Other Books By Lumos Learning For High School

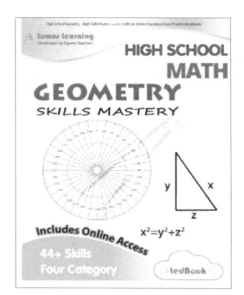

Available

- At Leading book stores
- www.lumoslearning.com/a/lumostedbooks

Made in the USA
Middletown, DE
23 June 2023